THE LAST DAYS OF EUROPE

ALSO BY WALTER LAQUEUR

Young Germany:
A History of the German Youth Movement (1962)

Russia and Germany: A Century of Conflict (1965)

Europe Since Hitler (1970)

A History of Zionism (1972)

Weimar: A Cultural History, 1918–1933 (1974)

Terrorism (1977)

A Continent Astray: Europe, 1970–1978 (1979)

Farewell to Europe: A Novel (1981)

The Terrible Secret: Suppression of the Truth About Hitler's "Final Solution" (1981, 1998)

Breaking the Silence (1986; with Richard Breitman)

The Age of Terrorism (1987)

The Long Road to Freedom: Russia and Glasnost (1989)

Thursday's Child Has Far to Go:
A Memoir of the Journeying Years (1992)

Black Hundred: The Rise of the Extreme Right in Russia (1993)

Fascism: Past, Present, Future (1996)

Guerrilla Warfare: A Historical and Critical Study (1997)

The New Terrorism:
Fanaticism and the Arms of Mass Destruction (1999)

No End to War: Terrorism in the Twenty-first Century (2003)

Voices of Terror: Manifestos, Writings, and Manuals of Al Qaeda, Hamas, and Other Terrorists from Around the World and Throughout the Ages (2004)

The Changing Face of Anti-Semitism (2006)

Dying for Jerusalem:
The Past, Present, and Future of the Holiest City (2006)

THE LAST DAYS OF
EUROPE

Epitaph for an
Old Continent

WALTER LAQUEUR

Thomas Dunne Books/St. Martin's Press New York

To Avi and Aaron,

great-grandsons born into this century

THOMAS DUNNE BOOKS.
An imprint of St. Martin's Press.

Book design by Richard Oriolo

ISBN-13: 978-0-312-36870-8
ISBN-10: 0-312-36870-4

Book Club Edition

Contents

Preface

MY MEMORIES OF EUROPE GO back to a childhood in Weimar Germany and the Nazi Third Reich, and I have been regularly commuting between Europe and America for slightly more than forty years. I have been to most European countries, and they have been my field of study for much of the time. My children went to school on both sides of the Atlantic, my work has been on both sides, too, and I have owned homes in both America and Europe, sometimes a great convenience, at others the cause of great problems.

True, I know some parts of the continent better than others, and the same refers to my knowledge of its main languages. I have not been to the Balkans, and there are aspects of European history and culture of which I am woefully ignorant. I have seen Europe and the Europeans in good times and bad. After all this, the time may have come for a summing up, as the Europe I have known is in the process of disappearing. What will take its place? The general direction seems to be clear, and it is not one that fills my heart with great joy. Nor do I have answers to the great problems that will face Europe in the years to come. I envy those who have written in recent years about Europe's brilliant future. I wish I could share their optimism. I suspect it will be a modest future. I hope it will be more than that of a museum.

WALTER LAQUEUR
Washington, D.C., and London,
December 2006

THE LAST DAYS OF EUROPE

Introduction

A Very Brief Trip Through
a Future Europe

IF A FRIEND or a cousin from abroad came to London thirty years ago and asked to see what was new in the British capital, where would we have taken him? Not an easy decision—the Barbican perhaps, about to become a cultural center, arts unlimited, galleries, home of the Royal Shakespeare Theatre, as well as countless restaurants, pubs, and bars. Or perhaps to Canary Wharf, once the West India docks and cargo warehouses, but about to become the new business and banking center. "Vibrant" was the term to be used. Even a new city airport was planned there in the middle of town.

If the scene was Paris, we would have shown him the Centre Pompidou opened in 1977 near the big indoor market in the fourth arrondissement, not very fashionable (and the exposed pipes an eyesore), but the place where the action was, with fifty thousand works of art—not all on display, needless to say. Or we would have taken him to La Défense, a new business center with many sky-scrapers, the impressive La Grande Arche and Palace, quite differ-ent from earlier such quarters. In Berlin we would have shown him the Wall, but this was not really that new. If our friend was inter-ested in architecture, the choice was clear—the Maerkische Viertel and the buildings designed by Walter Gropius.

Today the decision would be easier. We could show him Berlin Mitte with the new ministries, the center of the new capital. But Berlin has been a capital before with a lot of ministries from the Wilhelmstrasse to the Bendlerstrasse. If our friend really wanted to see the future, we would not have to rely on lengthy ex-planations and abstract description—a short walk or bus ride would do in order to get a preview of the shape of things to come. An excellent starting point would be Neukölln or Cottbusser Tor in Berlin, or Saint-Denis or Evry in the Paris *banlieues*. In some ways moving about has become much easier. There are fewer language difficulties; the argot of the *banlieues (verlan)*, we are told by *Le Monde,* consists of four hundred words. True, in Kreuzberg (also locally known as SO 36—the old postal code) a knowledge of Turkish could be more helpful than talking German. Among the younger generation Kanakensprach, consisting of three hundred words (part fecal, part sexual in origin), is probably even more useful. (For a taste see the translation of "Snow White" and "Hansel and Gretel" into Kanakensprach on the Web site of Detlev Mahnert.) In Britain, hip-hop language, an interesting mixture of materialism and nihilism, also has a great deal to do with violence and pit bulls; its origins are Jamaican but hardly Islamic.

In London we would stroll along Edgware Road, starting at Marble Arch, or, if our visitor wanted to venture farther afield, we would take a bus to Tower Hamlets (the old East End) or Lambeth, where the archbishop has his official residence, or to Lewisham. If our visitor had a special interest in Southeast Asia, we would take him to Brent in the north; if he is interested in things African, we would take a taxi to Peckham.

These parts offer much of interest, and the guidebooks recommend their gastronomic delights. The sounds of Cairo (minus the architecture) and the sights and smells of Karachi and Dacca can be found in these areas. A few of these quarters will strike the visitor as threatening (more perhaps in Paris than in London and Berlin), but many are quite charmingly exotic, the women in black in their *hijab;* the halal butchers, the kebab palaces, and the couscous eating places enriching the menus of the local restaurants, the Aladdin cafés and the Marhaba minimarkets. The visitor will be offered *fattoush* and falafel, and he will soon realize that Mecca Cola has replaced Coca-Cola in these parts. Many of the placards and inscriptions are in languages and alphabets he cannot read (unless he happens to be a graduate of the nearby School of Oriental Studies).

The corner shops sell Arab, Bengali, and Urdu newspapers in London and Turkish ones in Berlin. The visitor will pass by mosques, though not that many, since most are in side streets or in the suburbs. In West Ham, near the new Olympic stadium, they are building a new one to accommodate forty thousand faithful for prayer. Some cities now have more mosques than churches— Birmingham, for instance, and Bradford. The churches are bigger but much emptier. He will pass by cultural centers and clubs financed by the government of Saudi Arabia or sometimes by Libya. There are bookshops selling religious treatises but also secular literature. Sometimes from under the counter, militant pamphlets will be produced, considered hate literature by the misguided infidels.

Edgware Road is an interesting social mixture; Church Street Market with its fruit and vegetable stalls is certainly not a place where the wealthy shop; they do so at Harrods in Knightsbridge, which belongs to an Egyptian. But the Lamborghinis and the Ferraris to be seen and heard here in the evenings belong to young Arabs. The Maroush restaurant is certainly not inexpensive, and the Arab and North African pop stars and the belly dancers are well paid. Widely used are hookas, the water pipes (called shishas or narghiles in Berlin). There are few Maseratis in the streets of Kreuzberg, but there is a restaurant named Bagdad in the Schlesische Strasse.

Music is an essential part of this scene with Abdel Ali Sliman in London and Cheb Khaled in Paris. The French rappers doing their *rai* were first on the scene (in Bobigny in 1984 to be precise), but they perform almost exclusively for their compatriots, whereas in London young Englishmen and -women also attend these sessions. There is less music in Kreuzberg, which in contrast to the Paris *banlieues* is still ethnically mixed. (But there are hard-core rappers in Turkish Berlin, too.) There is a political-cultural contradiction here because the Muslim fundamentalists, above all the Muslim Brotherhood (founded in Egypt in 1928), are strictly opposed to musical entertainment, not to mention the belly dancers. But if the fundamentalists would try to impose their will in these parts of Paris and London, the preachers would lose much of their popularity. The rappers of the *banlieues* have more followers among the young than do the imams; they refer to Islam, Allah, and Muhammad in their music (often to the dismay of the preachers). Some of the rappers predicted the riots of 2005, while others called for calm.

All this is a far cry from what these quarters used to be in the 1950s and '60s when they were British or French or German working-class neighborhoods. The locals have mostly moved out and some of the neighborhoods have become a little more colorful (less in Paris than in London). Wedding in Berlin used to be a communist stronghold and its song

> *Left, left, left, left*
> *the red Wedding is marching*

about the class struggle and antifascism was known all over Germany. Today it is a dumping place for the rubbish in the middle of the German capital and some tell me that no one in his right mind will walk its streets at night alone. Once upon a time the red *banlieue* was the stronghold of the French Communists, but these days, too, have gone.

Such visits are an educational experience, but folkloristic interest quite apart, it is also a glance into the future. For these quarters are spreading, and within a generation they will cover a much greater area of the big cities of Europe, a gradual process that can be observed, for instance, in Berlin's Tiergarten or Moabit sections. In what direction will these quarters expand? In London, west of Edgware Road is Bayswater, but this has been Arab and Middle Eastern territory for a long time, south is Hyde Park, and to the west the West End with its elegant and expensive shops. The Middle

Eastern upper crust moved long ago to Knightsbridge and Kensington, not far from their embassies. In Berlin there is no Turkish upper class, only a middle class. Small for the time being, they have been moving to certain streets in Schöneberg but also to Charlottenburg and other parts in the west, but there are no Turkish middle-class concentrations.

True, northern parts of Neukölln have been embellished and apartments there are no longer cheap; in the same way, you may have to pay close to a million dollars for an apartment on the Isle of Dogs (Seacon Towers, for instance), which is also part of London's East End. But those settling in these gentrified areas are likely to be British yuppies rather than of Pakistani or Turkish origin.

THERE WILL BE GREAT CHANGES in the cities of Europe within the next decades. Will they be all one-sided, affecting only the natives and not at all the newcomers? Perhaps the Muslim women will opt for colors other than black, and perhaps the *hijab* will be reduced to something more symbolic? Perhaps their predilection for couscous will give way to fish and chips and bockwurst? (And if it does not, what harm will be done?) Perhaps mosque attendance will drop just as church attendance did in Western Europe. Is the attractive power of the European way of life so small that it will be overwhelmed by foreign customs and habits? Could it not be that the new immigrants stick to their old ways imported from Anatolia or North Africa or Pakistani villages precisely because they still are a minority, fearful of losing their identity, and could it be that once they feel no longer under siege but constitute a majority their societies might open up to outside influence irrespective of the warnings of their religious leaders?

A hundred years ago, a visit to Commercial Road in London's East End, or to the Grenadierstrasse and the Scheunenviertel in East Berlin or Belleville and the Marais in Paris or the Lower East Side in New York City, would have shown a scenery that was quite strange and not particularly pleasing to the eye. You would have seen the Jewish immigrants from Eastern Europe in their new European or American surroundings: the little synagogues, the cheap eating places, the sweatshops; the foreign-language newspapers; the men and women in strange, outlandish clothes.

But there are differences. There is, to begin with, the *scale* of immigration. Only tens of thousands came to Western Europe at the time, not millions. They made great efforts to integrate socially and culturally. Above all, they wanted to give their children a good secular education at almost any price. The rate of intermarriage was high within one generation and even higher within two. No one helped them, there were no social workers or advisers, no one gave them housing at low or no rent, and programs such as Sure Start (a British equivalent of Head Start) and "positive discrimination" had not yet been invented. There was no free health service or unemployment benefits. There was no social safety net—it was a question of swimming or sinking. There were no government committees analyzing Judeophobia and how to combat it.

The immigrant Jews entered trade and the professions and their social rise was quick and spectacular. They made a significant contribution to the cultural and scientific life of their adopted countries. A few strove to maintain the old way of life of the Eastern European shtetl, but the majority wanted assimilation and acculturation.

Many of the immigrants of 2006 live in societies separate from those of the host countries. This is true for big cities and small. They have no German or British or French friends, they do not meet them, and frequently they do not speak their language. Their preachers tell these immigrants that their values and traditions are greatly superior to those of the infidels and that any contact with them, even with neighbors, is undesirable. Their young people complain about being victims and being excluded, but their social and cultural separateness is quite often voluntary. Western European governments and societies are often criticized for not having done more to integrate these new citizens. But even if they had done much more, is it certain that integration would have succeeded? For integration is not a one-sided affair.

Do these immigrants identify with their new homeland? If you ask them, they will frequently tell you that they are Muslims (or Turks or Nigerians) living in Britain, France, or Germany. They get their politics, religion, and culture from Arab and Turkish television channels. They may identify on the local level, rooting for a hometown soccer club such as Hertha BSC or Liverpool. If Germany plays Sweden, as during the recent world championship, they will hoist in Berlin the Turkish and the German flags. But if France is playing Algeria, the boys from the *banlieues* will boo "The Marseillaise" and applaud the North African team. However, they have no wish to go back to Turkey or Algeria—this is their country and they show it; no one should have any doubt about it.

To what extent are these degrees of separateness and identification likely to change in the years to come? These are some of the questions that will be addressed in the following pages.

The Last Days of Old Europe

"THE LAST DAYS of Old Europe"—a few words of clarification are called for. "The last days" is, of course, a figure of speech; there is

no volcano, to the best of my knowledge, about to erupt and bury
the continent overnight as at Pompeii and Herculaneum. There is a
danger of the level of the oceans rising and coastal towns being
flooded, but this is not a specifically European threat. On the sur-
face, everything seems almost normal, even attractive. But Europe
as we knew it is bound to change, probably out of recognition for a
number of reasons, partly demographic-cultural, but also because
of political-social reasons. Even if Europe should unite and solve
the various domestic crises facing it, its predominant place in the
world (the "navel of the world") and predominant role in world affairs is a thing of the past, and the predictions of the emergence of
Europe as a moral superpower are bound to remain an engaging
fantasy.

"Old Europe" is not a term invented by former U.S. defense
secretary Donald Rumsfeld but appeared in the first half of the
nineteenth century, at the time of the Congress of Vienna and the
publication of *The Communist Manifesto* (1848), but I do not refer to
this historic usage or to the well-known restaurant on Wisconsin
Avenue in Washington, D.C. (known for its sauerbraten and variety
of sausages).

"Old Europe" in the present context refers to the European
Community (formerly the EEC—the European Economic Community), but including Russia and the other parts of the former
Soviet Union situated west of the Urals. What kind of new Europe
is likely to emerge as a successor to the old continent? This, of
course, is an open question whose answer depends on events not
only in Europe but also in other parts of the world.

Given the shrinking of its population, it is possible that Europe, or at any case considerable parts of it, will turn into a cultural
theme park, a kind of Disneyland on a level of a certain sophistication for well-to-do visitors from China and India, something like
Brugge, Venice, Versailles, Stratford-on-Avon, or Rothenburg ob

der Tauber on a larger scale. Some such parks already exist; when the coal mines in the Ruhr were closed down, the Warner Brothers Movie World was opened in Dortmund, which presents not only Batman but also the Agfa museum of German film history. More than that, Essen was selected in March 2006 as the European capital of culture for 2010; former cultural capitals of Europe have been Glasgow and Antwerp.

This will be a Europe of tourist guides, gondoliers, and translators: "Ladies and gentlemen, you are visiting the scenes of a highly developed civilization that once led the world. It gave us Shakespeare, Beethoven, the welfare state, and many other fine things. . . ." There will be excursions for every taste; even now there are trips in Berlin to the slums and the areas considered dangerous ("Kreuzberg, the most colorful district: two hours").

This scenario may appear somewhat fanciful at the moment, but given current trends it is a possibility that cannot be dismissed out of hand. Tourism has been of paramount importance in Switzerland for a long time; it is now of great (and growing) importance in France, Italy, Spain, Greece, Portugal, and some other countries. Tourism's average growth rate across Europe is 4 percent annually. In several European countries it is becoming the most important single factor in the economy and the main earner of foreign exchange. By now the Chinese are the biggest-spending visitors in Paris, and this is only the beginning.

It is equally possible that having solved one way or another its internal social and economic problems and being able to compete again in the world markets, getting its political act together at least to some degree, Europe will find a place in the new world order likely to emerge, more modest than in the past but still respectable.

This is the best-case scenario, but it is also possible that the general decline and deterioration may continue and even become more pronounced. European conditions under the impact of massive waves of immigration could become similar to those prevailing in North Africa and the Middle East. These and perhaps some other scenarios in between the extremes seem possible at the current time. What appears impossible is that the twenty-first century will be the European century, as some observers, mainly in the United States, claimed even a few years ago. As they saw it, a united Europe not only had caught up with the U.S. economy but also was likely to overtake it very soon. The countries of Europe were living in peace with one another and their neighbors; they had established a way of life, a model, more civilized and humane than any other. True, it was not exactly a political-military superpower, but through its "transformative power" acting as an example, it was changing the world. In brief, the rest of the world was becoming more and more like Europe, moving toward an order that was more just and humane than any in the annals of mankind.

But Europe did not move closer together, and it did not catch up and overtake America. On the contrary, it found it more and more difficult to compete with China and India. The character of power in world politics did not radically change and the predictions of yesterday seemed more and more detached from the facts of the real world. And the question inevitably arose how such hallucinations could have arisen in the first place.

Looking back thirty, even fifteen years, *extenuating* circumstances could be found for engaging in what now appear mere pipe dreams. To give a personal example: A history of postwar Europe by the present writer, first published in the 1970s, appeared in the 1990s (in translation) under the title "Europe on the Road to Being a World Power"—and while nonfiction titles are often given by publishers rather than authors, I did not protest. I did not protest because the recovery of Europe after World War II was spectacular, in some ways even miraculous. In 1945, as the guns fell silent, many thought that Europe was finished and would never recover. But recover it did, and within a decade the various economic miracles took place. The recovery was not only economic. Not only were European living standards higher than ever before, but also welfare states were established providing essential health services, free education, and other services; no one any longer had to fear disease, old age, and unemployment. European countries lived in peace with one another, borders were gradually removed, and there was no war or danger of war—except perhaps on the borderlands of Europe such as the Balkans.

Europe had been divided during the cold war, the Berlin Wall came down with the collapse of the Soviet empire, and the countries of Eastern Europe became free. Seen in retrospect, there was much reason for optimism. True, Europe had not reemerged as a major player in world affairs but had to rely on soft power with all its limitations. However, it had made great progress toward close cooperation. Common institutions had emerged, and there seemed reason to believe that given a few more years there would be a common European foreign and defense policy, so that the old continent would again play a role in world affairs commensurate with its history and its economic power.

There were danger signs even in the 1970s when the great boom slowed down and unemployment began to appear. The terms "Euroscepticism" and "Eurosclerosis" go back to the late 1980s, but they referred to the rigidity of the European labor market and, generally speaking, to the economic situation with its ups and downs rather than to Europe's political future. It was only in later years that a significant change in European attitudes took place. Progress toward further unification stalled despite the introduction of a common currency, the euro, and other seemingly important measures. But the European enthusiasm that had once been so startling and positive declined.

More important yet, there were warning demographic signs. Europe was not reproducing itself, the experts claimed in the late 1980s. But these warnings were not taken seriously by officials because they referred to long-term trends and governments in Europe (like governments elsewhere) were elected for a few years only. Nor did the general public pay much attention, even though no specialized training in statistics and demography was needed to realize that important changes were taking place; a walk in the cities of Europe showed the simple fact that there were far fewer children around than in the past. Some argued that demographers had been wrong with their predictions in the past; even in the 1960s many not only in the world at large but also in Europe had predicted that the great danger facing mankind was *overpopulation*. The general public took even less notice of these warnings—some for ideological reasons, believing that the world was already overpopulated and that as a result the equilibrium of nature had been damaged. But the great majority with no ideological agendas simply ignored these changes because the danger (if a danger it was) seemed remote and uncertain.

The experts were sounding the tocsin in the 1990s. A number of works by Alfred Sauvy, the best-known French demographer of his generation, and his disciple Jean-Claude Chesnais attracted some attention (see Chesnais, *The Twilight of the Occident* [1995] and *Revenge of the Third World* [1987], and Sauvy, *The Aging of Nations* [2000]). As Chesnais put it, Europe was old and rigid, so it was fading. One could see this as the natural cycle of civilization, perhaps an inevitable development. In Germany the studies of Herwig Birg, a distinguished professor and head of the professional organization of German demographers, at long last got a hearing with his work *Die demographische Zeitenwende* (The Demographic Turning Point in History), which in turn inspired a leading journalist, Frank Schirrmacher, who published the *Methusalem Komplott* (The Methuselah Conspiracy), discussing the problems of a graying society, which for many months headed the German bestseller list.

In Russia dark predictions were made—above all in far right-wing circles in the 1980s—concerning the future of the Russian and Ukrainian peoples; the specter of alcoholism (a very real one) was conjured up. Attention was drawn to the fact that fewer and fewer children were being born, that there was a mass flight from the countryside, and that life expectancy (especially of men) in the Soviet Union was steadily declining. But even to this day Russia has not fully awakened to its demographic prospects.

It should have been clear that the face and the character of Europe were changing. There had been guest workers, millions of them, who played a vital role in the economic miracle of the 1950s. But these had been mainly Europeans: Italians, Spaniards, Portuguese, and Yugoslavs who eventually returned to their countries of origin. They were replaced by millions of new immigrants from Asia, the Middle East, and Africa; many of them had come as political asylum seekers but in fact had been in search of a better life for themselves and their children. Unlike the earlier guest workers, they had no intention of returning to their homelands. But many of them also had no desire to integrate into European societies the way earlier immigrant waves had done. This resistance to assimilation created increasing social, political, and cultural problems, which were considered manageable until, at about the turn of the millennium, it was suddenly realized that these newcomers constituted about a quarter (sometimes a third) of the population of the inner quarters of many European cities. They were a majority among the youngest generation; in Brussels, for instance, as of 2004 more than 55 percent of the children born were of immigrant parents. In the Ruhr region in Germany, within a few years more than half of the cohort under thirty will be of non-German origin. In the foreseeable future, perhaps in the lifetime of many of those attending kindergarten now, non-Germans will constitute the majority. Thus almost overnight what had been considered a minor problem on a local level is becoming a major political issue, for there is growing resistance on the part of the native population, who resent becoming strangers in their own homelands. Perhaps they are wrong to react in this way, but they have not been aware until recently of this trend, and no one ever asked or consulted them.

In brief, by the turn of the millennium, at the very latest, it should have been clear that Europe was no longer on the road to superpower status, but that it faced an existential crisis—or, perhaps more accurately, a number of major crises, of which the demographic problem was the most severe. This began to be recognized almost immediately, but again there was confusion because the crisis seemed intractable—it had been discovered too late. One could only hope that the newcomers indifferent to European values or even hostile to them would gradually show more tolerance, if not enthusiasm, toward them or that multiculturalism, which had been such a disappointment, would perhaps work after all in the long run.

These were not exactly strong hopes, and they certainly do not explain the illusions of some foreign observers who continued to claim that the twenty-first century would be Europe's. They claimed that there had been a revolution in Europe of which most Americans had not even been aware. Europe had a vision of justice and harmony very much in contrast to the American dream, which no longer existed. The European vision emphasized the collective, in contrast to the narrow stress on individualism in the United States. It preferred the quality of life to amassing money. Americans had to work harder than Europeans, had fewer holidays, did not live as long as the Europeans, and, generally speaking, enjoyed life much less. If Goethe had once said *"Amerika, du hast es besser* [America, you are better off]," this was no longer true at all. Europeans were selfless, it was argued; according to a recent poll, 95 percent of them had said that altruism, the wish to help others, was their highest value. Or, as another observer put it, power politics was a thing of the past; Europe's main weapon was justice and the law. Coming from Europe, this idea would spread all over the world and would become the main instrument in world politics.

I AM NOT CONCERNED HERE, however, with comparisons between America and Europe, the merits and demerits of their respective ways of life, but with the state of Europe, on which the American friends of Europe, it would soon appear, were sadly misinformed. How to explain the depth of such confusion? The motivation and their underlying assumptions were different; they had much more to do with the situation in America than with the European realities. Tony Judt, author of a massive history of postwar Europe, wrote about Europe's emergence in the dawn of the twenty-first century as a paragon of the international virtues: a community of values and a system of interstate relations held up by Europeans and non-Europeans as an example for all to emulate. In part this was the backwash of growing disillusion with the American alternative.

The praises of Europe and the rosy prophecies that in retrospect seem so misplaced were written by critics of the foreign and domestic policy of the United States and in particular of the administration of George W. Bush. Whether their critique of the United States was correct or not is irrelevant in this context; what matters is the psychological motivation. They came to see in Europe all (or at least many of) the things they were missing in America and came to believe not only that the European model was preferable but also that it was going to prevail. As Mark Leonard wrote in a book titled *Why Europe Will Run the 21st Century* (2005), "As this process continues we will see the emergence of a 'New European Century.' Not because Europe will run the world as an empire but because the European way of doing things will have become the world's." And the slightly more cautious Tony Judt: "The twenty-first century may yet belong to Europe." Their deeply held convictions about the state of America apparently blinded them to the seriousness of the European crisis. They failed to understand that their image of postwar Europe was a thing of the past. True, by 2006 some of them, such as Charles Kupchan, had retreated from their former optimism, but others had not. There was still a strange fixation on the rivalry between Europe and America, ignoring the fact that other centers of power were emerging that constituted a major challenge and also very serious competition.

But it would be unfair to focus on the imperfect knowledge or understanding of some American observers. The illusions were shared by many leading political figures in Europe. As the year 2000 was solemnly rung in as befitted the beginning of a new century and millennium, it often seemed business as usual. It was the last year of Bill Clinton's presidency in the United States, in Russia Vladimir Putin was elected, Greece joined the European Union, and Slobodan Milošević was overthrown. A few disasters occurred, such as the tragic loss of the Russian submarine *Kursk* and the explosion of a Concorde at Charles de Gaulle Airport in Paris. Real Madrid won the European soccer championship, and for the first time in history Spain won the Davis Cup in tennis.

At the end of March that year, heads of European Union governments and prime ministers met in Lisbon to discuss their strategy for the next ten years. Among the main issues at stake were full employment and the encouragement of European research and innovation. The general consensus was that Europe would become the most competitive and dynamic economy in the world, able to sustain permanent growth with more and better places of work and greater social cohesion. This, as was stated in the final communiqué, could be achieved through the transition to a European economy and society based on science, the modernization of the European model, the investment in human beings, and combating social marginalization. All schools should have access to the Internet and multimedia by the end of the year 2001, workers should be taxed less, peace should prevail in the Balkans, and a political solution should be found for Chechnya. Altogether, 28 main targets were defined and 120 secondary aims projected. Nothing was said in the Lisbon resolutions about demography and the growing tensions with the immigrant communities.

One could not deny that the delegates had brought vision and ambition to the Lisbon deliberations. But they were remote from European realities. It could well have been that the Lisbon declarations were unduly influenced by the false dawn of 2000, for this particular year was an exceptional one for European economic growth, which reached 3 percent, much higher than during the years before and after. When five years later the statesmen met again for an interim review, they had to admit that progress had been very limited, and even this assessment understated the reality, for unemployment had grown and labor productivity had not been significantly increased. There had been no quantum jump as expected, and the chances to become the most dynamic sphere in the world economy seemed more remote than ever. True, the Europe of fifteen nations had become a Europe of twenty-five. But it had not become a more closely knit union. On the contrary, the centrifugal trends had become stronger, as seen in the vote against a common European constitution, first in France and later in Holland (both referendums in 2005). This came as a great surprise and shock to the Brussels Eurocrats but also to a considerable part of the political class in Europe because it did not conform to their vision of Europe. There was bound to be a rude awakening. One seemed further than ever from a common European foreign and defense policy. The earlier Euro-optimism had given way to a wave of pessimism, the expression not just of a changing mood but of the belated realization that the continent faced enormous problems with which it had not yet come to terms: that the issue at stake was not its emergence as the leading superpower but survival. Official Brussels still believed that the European Union of 2020 would look much as it did when *Europe's World* was published in the summer of 2006. But even if that should turn out to be true, it left open the question of how the rest of the world would look that year and what the specific weight of Europe would be in that world.

ONE

Europe
Shrinking

MY MATERNAL GRANDFATHER, A MILLER, was born in 1850 and lived in Upper Silesia. He had six children. Three of his six children had no children of their own, two had two each, and one had a single child. This, in a nutshell, is the story of the rise and decline of the population of Europe. The average European family had five children in the nineteenth century, but this number declined steadily until it fell below the reproduction rate (2.2) in the major European countries before the outbreak of World War I. There were brief periods when the trend went in the opposite direction, for instance the baby boom after World War II, when the birthrate in all European countries rose above 2.2 and in some nations, such as the Netherlands, Ireland, and Portugal, above 3.0. But this lasted for less than a decade, and since the late 1950s the decline has continued. At present the total fertility rate for Europe is 1.37. (The crude birthrate is the number of births per 1,000 persons per year.) To give another example, in Italy and in Spain in the early years of the twenty-first century, about half as many children were born as around 1960. This trend continues, and it is difficult to think why there should be a lasting reversal. In a hundred years the population of Europe will be only a fraction of what it is today, and in two hundred years some countries may have disappeared.

It is certainly a striking trend considering that only a hundred years ago Europe was the center of the world. Africa consisted almost entirely of European colonies, and India was the jewel of the British empire. Germany, France, and Russia had the strongest armies in the world, Britain the strongest navy. The European economy was leading the world. America was making rapid progress, but it still had a long way to go, and few were taking notice. Politically and culturally, only London and Paris, Berlin and Vienna counted; there was no good reason that European students should attend American universities, which were behind the European in every respect.

But there were clouds on the horizon, for instance the Russian revolution of 1905. But in Russia, too, there was considerable economic progress. There were tensions between the European powers, but there had been no war for several decades, and a war seemed unlikely. The confidence of Europe was unbroken. The world population in 1900 was about 1.7 billion, of whom one out of four lived in Europe. Europe's population was about six times that of the United States, which was 76 million at the time. Then World War I broke out with its horrible devastation and its many millions of victims—some 8.5 million soldiers died and 13 million civilians perished from starvation, disease, and massacres— followed by revolutions, civil war, inflation, and mass unemployment. Europe had become considerably weaker, but it was still the center of the world, the leading force.

All the while the population clock was ticking away, but few paid attention because in absolute figures the population of Europe continued to increase, and people were living longer. But Europe's numbers grew much more slowly than the population in other parts of the world. If the population of Europe had been 422 million in the year 1900, it was 548 million in 1950 and 727 million in 2000. In fact, there were false alarms from time to time of overpopulation. When I went to school in Germany (beginning before the Nazi takeover), the teachers talked at great length about the need for more lebensraum, "living space." The famous bestseller of that period was Hans Grimm's *Volk ohne Raum* (A People Without Space). The author had lived for many years in South Africa, and he thought, like many others, that agriculture was the most important pillar of the national economy and determined the health of the nation. This was wrong even at the time (before the great technological revolution in agriculture), and Hitler, too, had accepted that for building up and maintaining a big, modern army developing heavy industry was more important than growing potatoes and tomatoes. But even after World War II the fairy tale of European overpopulation found for a while influential supporters such as the Club of Rome, which published 30 million copies of a report in 1972 about the limits of growth that preached precisely this warning about overpopulation.

What was the reason for the steady decline of the birthrate in

Europe? This is a question not easy to answer because the trend took place all over the continent—in countries of very different character in north and south, in west and east, in Catholic and Protestant and Orthodox countries, among the very rich and the relatively poor. For this reason it does not come as a surprise that there is no unanimity among demographers on this question. The birth control pill played a certain role but probably not a decisive one. More important was the fact that more and more women accepted (or felt compelled to accept) working full-time and did not want their careers interrupted by pregnancies and the need to take care of their babies. To give but one example, half of the female scientists in Germany are childless. Most important in all probability was the fact that the institution of the family had greatly declined in value and esteem. Families became outmoded; many wanted to enjoy themselves, not to be tied down by all kinds of obligations and responsibilities. Thus the apparent paradox that at the very time when Europeans could afford to have more children than at any time in the past they had many fewer children.

Given this decline, what are the predictions for the future? According to the estimates of the United Nations and the European Community ("World Population Prospects" and "Eurostat"), the population of France will decline only slightly, from about 60 million at present to 55 million in 2050 and 43 million at the end of the century, but the number of ethnic French will decline rapidly. A similar trend is forecast for the United Kingdom: from 60 million at present to 53 million in 2050 and 45 million in 2100. Most other European countries would fare considerably worse. Thus the population of Germany, 82 million at present, will decline to 61 million in 2050 and 32 million in 2100. The decline of Italy and Spain would be drastic. Italy counts some 57 million inhabitants at present; this is expected to shrink to 37 million at midcentury and 15 million by 2100. The figures for Spain are 39 million at present, declining to 28 million in 2050 and 12 million at the end of the century. All these predictions do not take into account immigration in the decades to come.

The projected population losses for Eastern Europe for midcentury are even more catastrophic:

Ukraine: 43 percent
Bulgaria: 34 percent
Latvia and Lithuania: 25–27 percent
Russian Federation: 22 percent
Croatia: 20 percent
Hungary: 18 percent
Czech Republic: 17 percent

By 2050, according to these sources, only Cyprus, Luxembourg, Malta, and perhaps Sweden will still be growing. This is only part of the overall picture, however. For once societies become overage, the number of those able to produce children falls rapidly and the decline gathers momentum. For the first time in history there are more people aged over sixty than under twenty in major European countries such as Italy, Germany, Spain, and Greece. The other factor that has to be taken into account is that the relatively slow decline in countries such as France and Britain will be the result of the relatively high fertility rate among the immigrant communities—black and North African in France and Pakistani and Caribbean in Britain.

It is true that there has been a worldwide decline in fertility; the fertility rate has halved, broadly speaking, in the third world from 6.2 children to 3.4 between 1965 and 2000, and, according to UN and other projections, the world population in 2100 will be approximately 8 billion and then decline. (It is 6 billion at present.) However, in the regions closest to Europe such as North Africa, sub-Saharan Africa, and the Middle East, there will be no decline in the near future. According to these projections, the population of Turkey will be 100 million in 2050, that of Egypt 114 million, and there will be 45 million Algerians and 45 million Moroccans. The highest rise will be in the very poorest countries. By 2050 Yemen will have a larger population than the Russian Federation and Nigeria and Pakistan will each have a larger population than the fifteen nations comprising until recently the European Community. Germany, at present the fourteenth most populous country, will have fallen behind Congo, Ethiopia, Uganda, Vietnam, Turkey, Egypt, Afghanistan, and Kenya.

Russia has at present a population of 145 million, but it will be overtaken first by Turkey and subsequently by many other countries, including perhaps even Yemen and Ethiopia. Yemen (as Paul Demeny pointed out in an article in *Population and Development Review* in 2003), which had about 4 million inhabitants in 1950, has now some 20 million and, according to the projections based on current fertility rates, will have more than a hundred million by 2050. At the same time, the population of Russia is shrinking annually by 2 percent, which is to say that within fifty years its population will shrink to one-third of its current size. Demeny observes that there is hardly any precedent for such a precipitous demographic collapse in human history.

Common sense finds it difficult to accept such projections, and for good reasons—not so much with regard to the Russian demographic collapse but concerning the growth of Yemen. Yemen is a poor country, much of its territory consists of desert (only 3 percent of the country is arable), and there is little water. The prospects for agriculture are limited, and while a certain amount of industrialization will no doubt take place, the idea that the Yemen economy could sustain a population of more than 100 million defies even the most fertile imagination. It seems more than likely that the population of Yemen (and of other countries in a similar position) will grow less, because there will be neither work nor food. Similar considerations apply to Egypt. But at the same time it seems certain that even if there were to be a dramatic decrease in the Yemeni fertility rate, the population of that country will considerably increase, many will look for work outside their native country, and there will be far greater population pressure on Europe. For more fortunate countries such as Turkey, however, the projections for 2050 and beyond seem quite realistic. And it also seems quite realistic that Europe's share in the world population will be no more than 4 to 5 percent in 2050, in the lifetime of many of those living now, having been 25 percent in 1900 and 12 percent in 1950.

The same considerations apply to projections beyond the year 2100. According to the UN projections for the year 2300, the population of Europe will have fallen to a mere 59 million. Many European countries will be reduced to about 5 percent of their current population and Russia and Italy to 1 percent, less than live at present in the cities of Novosibirsk or Turin, respectively. While such a possibility cannot be ruled out, projections for long periods almost two hundred years into the future cannot possibly take into account scientific and technological developments. We do not know what progress medicine will make or how long people will live in two hundred years. However, pandemics or wars or natural disasters may have an impact that cannot be calculated. We do not know the impact of new technologies on labor productivity—how much of a workforce will be needed to keep the economies going. New ideologies or religions may appear that could influence population growth or decline.

Some have argued that if Europe is still a continent of any

importance two hundred years from now, it will almost certainly be a black continent. Others have predicted that at the end of the twenty-first century Europe will be Islamic. Such predictions are based on the higher African and Middle Eastern birthrate on one hand and the need for massive immigration into Europe on the other. Since Europe will be graying even in the next few decades, younger workers will be needed to secure the survival in reasonable comfort of the older generation no longer active in the workforce.

According to a scenario presented in the UN report *Replacement Migration: Is It a Solution to Declining and Ageing Populations?* no fewer than 700 million immigrants will be needed for the period between 1995 and 2050 to restore the age balance. But such figures largely belong to the realm of fantasy, for it is not known how many workers will be needed, nor from whence they will come. India and China, too, are aging and the birthrate is falling even in Bangladesh. At present the European problem is unemployment among young immigrant workers and the fact that many of them lack the skills needed to be of assistance in the workforce. Many of the second generation have not done well in the European educational system, which means that this problem is not likely to disappear soon. And even if they had the necessary skills, it is not clear whether they would be willing to work (as it were) for the well-being of the senior citizens of a society with which they do not identify. It will be difficult enough to reach a generational contract within the European societies, let alone a contract including newcomers from abroad. That Europe will need immigrants from abroad goes without saying, but whether such immigrants with the qualifications needed will be at all available is not known.

It is doubtful whether Europe will be Muslim at the end of this century. This might be true with regard to some cities and provinces, and it goes without saying that the Muslim element will play a far greater role in European politics and society than at present. But it will not apply to the continent as a whole for a variety of reasons. In the first place, many of the new immigrants to Europe are not Muslim—they come from India and Southeast Asia, from tropical Africa, the West Indies, and other parts of the world (more about this later). And while it is true that Muslim immigrants have been very resistant to absorption and integration, it is not certain that this will continue with equal intensity for several generations. In other words, the meaning of individuals or a community being "Islamic" by the end of the twenty-first century is by no means clear; it is only a projection that could be altered by all kinds of factors. That Europe at the end of the century will be very different from present-day Europe goes without saying. For all one knows, the continent might be greatly diminished in stature and influence and in deep trouble. But it will not necessarily be predominantly Islamist.

IS THE SHRINKING OF POPULATION necessarily a bad thing? And to what extent do figures really matter? Is it not in some respects desirable, because the dangers of overpopulation are only too obvious? And don't civilized conditions prevail far more often in smaller European countries than in big ones? This may be quite true, but the problem facing Europe is how to prevent too sudden a decline, which would have enormous social and economic consequences.

When the welfare state was first introduced after World War II the population structure of European societies was quite different from that of the present; furthermore, life expectancy has risen considerably and will continue to rise. According to some experts, by 2060 the average life expectancy will be about one hundred years. These changes have a direct impact on the amount of social security that has to be paid, as well as on medical care, insurance, and other social services. The same problems face other developed countries, but they are particularly acute in Europe and will be even more acute in the future. Where will the additional funds come from? What happens to the economy once the population shrinks? Some tend to believe that the productivity of labor (and capital) will provide the additional funds, but this seems less likely as time goes by. It is far more likely that social services will be cut. For instance, the age when pensions are due, at present sixty-five in most European countries, may be increased and the sums paid out (at present up to 70 percent of the average income) may have to be reduced.

Steps in this direction have been taken in many European countries and have encountered bitter opposition, but those opposing the painful cuts have not been able to present realistic counterproposals.

The median age is at present only slightly higher in Europe than in the United States (thirty-seven as compared with thirty-five in America). However, according to projections, it will be thirty-six in America in 2050 and about fifty-three in Europe. America will be a much younger country, a fact that has not only economic, measurable statistical consequences but also, perhaps more important, political and psychological ramifications. Assuming that military forces will still be needed fifty years from now, the question arises where Europe's soldiers will be coming from—unless the age of recruits will be increased by twenty years or so.

There are other factors that cannot be measured; within a generation or two the institution of the family will be even further weakened. In Germany the sharp decline began with the Generation of 1968 and the Frankfurt School, with its Critical Theory, which belittled the function of the family from both a social and an economic point of view. But the family declined also in other societies in which the year 1968 was not an important turning point. One prominent economist said that *Homo economicus* would have no children. What are the consequences if young people find that with the disappearance of the family their parents are their only relations? It will probably be a much lonelier and sadder world. We do not know the answers to this and related questions.

Two questions remain to be answered, however briefly: Could the projections be wrong? And is it possible to reverse these trends if it is accepted that this is desirable?

Historical experience tends to show that "natalist policies" are not very successful, at least not in the long run. Under Hitler and Mussolini, and also under Stalin for a while, a higher birthrate was strongly promoted by the propaganda machines of these regimes and a variety of incentives were promised and given to large families. But this did not affect the long-term trend of the birthrate. East Germany under the Communist regime provided a great deal of services for working mothers, and many complained that after the fall of the Berlin Wall many of these services were discontinued. But again this had no lasting impact on the birthrate. Among democratic societies, France and Sweden adopted policies likely to reduce the financial burden of having children. These include parental leave for many months before and after the birth of the child (and promised job security), tax reduction, and cash payment and various other incentives, including the possibility of working part-time. Some have suggested that when two candidates apply for the same job, then, other things being equal, precedence should be given to a mother over a childless woman. Altogether, Sweden spent ten times more on such incentives than did countries like Italy and Spain. But after a short-lived upsurge, the number of births went down again—a decline attributed to a downturn in the economy. But in Italy, where the birthrate went down even more, on the contrary, *prosperity* was thought to be the reason for the decline. In brief, Sweden and France, which provided a variety of incentives to encourage childbearing, cannot serve as a model; the most that can be said is that if not for these measures the birthrate would have declined even more.

There probably will be minor ups and downs in the European birthrate in the years to come, but the basic trend is downward, and while a radical turn is always possible, it is difficult at the present time even to imagine its causes.

What can be predicted with near mathematical certainty is that the decline will continue at least up to the middle of this century, because if there are more deaths than births, a whole generation will be missing that could have produced children. By and large the predictions of the demographers have been accurate, with only a minor quotient of error. Their predictions are made on a best-case as well as a worst-case scenario, with an additional prediction in the middle. Thus, to give but one example, the highest projection for the world population by midcentury is 10.6 billion, the lowest 7.4, and the medium 8.9. But as far as Europe is concerned, even the best-case scenarios show a negative trend.

Migrations

UNTIL ABOUT THE YEAR 2000, most thinking about the future of Europe, political, social, economic, or cultural, ignored demography. A visit to a school could have acted as a corrective, but few politicians, sociologists, or philosophers tend to visit schools.

True, few countries in Europe were ever ethnically homogeneous, but the minorities within their borders were not very remote from one another in outlook, mentality, and origin; they had not come from distant countries or even continents. Before the First

World War the migration of Poles to western Germany and northern France or of Jews from Eastern Europe had been on a relatively small scale. Moreover, these new immigrants had been eager to adopt the values and the way of life of their new home countries. Quite frequently they even changed their names in order to be more easily integrated.

Immigration on a massive scale after World War II took place as the result of political-territorial changes—such as the expulsion of Germans from Eastern and southeastern Europe and then, ten years later, as the result of the economic miracle. But again the newcomers were mainly from inside Europe: Italians and Yugoslavs who went to Germany, and Spanish and Portuguese who came to France. But the great majority of these groups did not stay but returned to their countries of origin as the economic situation there improved. During this period, major European countries recruited workers abroad to do the work European workers were not willing or able to do.

The next wave of immigrants had mainly to do with the dissolution of empires—West Indians, Pakistanis, and Indians who went to Britain, Indians who had been expelled by Idi Amin from Uganda also settled in the United Kingdom, and North Africans migrated to France. There was also an influx of Turks, mainly to Germany and to a lesser extent to other European countries. But it was generally assumed that this was a temporary phenomenon, that these guest workers (as they were called) would return to their home countries after having made some money that would enable them to be economically active in their native towns or villages. In fact, however, only half of the 2 to 3 million guest workers who came to Northern Europe in the 1960s did return to their homelands. The others stayed on legally or illegally and in many cases brought relatives to join them, and the host governments were not willing to enforce the law against those who broke it. Thus major foreign communities came into being around the time when the economy was worsening after the oil crisis of 1973 and as unemployment increased.

European governments ceased to issue labor permits, and as a result the number of immigrants to Europe should have declined or even come to a standstill and the number of foreign workers should have decreased, but this did not happen. For, quite apart from the high birthrate of Asian and African and Middle Eastern immigrants, there were a number of reasons for the increase that had not been taken into account by the government planners. First, the number of dependents who were brought legally and illegally from countries such as Pakistan, Turkey, and North Africa was considerably larger than had been assumed. Second, illegal immigration increased considerably and became an organized business. Illegal immigrants were smuggled from the Middle East through the Balkans and Eastern Europe or across the Mediterranean to Italy, from North Africa by way of Spain and Italy. Dozens, perhaps hundreds, perished on sea and land on these journeys.

And then there are the asylum seekers. In 1983 there were a mere 80,000 of them; by 1992 their number had risen to 700,000 throughout Europe. In the beginning the authorities had been quite liberal in their approach, even though the majority of these immigrants, probably the great majority, were not political refugees but "economic immigrants" in search of a better life for themselves and their children. Among the political asylum seekers there were Islamists or even terrorists who were indeed in danger of being arrested in their native countries, but for reasons that had nothing to do with the struggle for democracy and freedom. As far as can be ascertained, some illegal immigrants and also asylum seekers were criminals and came to establish criminal gangs (specializing in the drug trade, prostitution, car theft, etc.) in their new home countries. There were some genuine political refugees among them, but all asylum seekers, whether legitimate or illegitimate, were supported by a powerful lobby, the human rights associations and churches that provided legal and other aid. They claimed that it was scandalous and in violation of elementary human rights to turn back new immigrants and that in case of doubt mercy should prevail.

Gradually, the attitude of the authorities became considerably less tolerant; entrance permits were often denied, but these rejections usually remained a dead letter. Because the asylum seekers from Africa and the Middle East had frequently destroyed their papers, claiming that they had been lost, their stories could seldom be verified, and once they had entered European territory it became virtually impossible to deport them. According to the Schengen accord (begun in 1985 in Schengen, Luxembourg, between that country and Belgium, the Netherlands, France, and Germany and later including other European nations), border controls inside Europe were largely abolished and if an immigrant had put foot into one European country he could move freely to another.

Germany was the target of most asylum seekers by far—some 2 million between 1990 and 2000—followed by the United Kingdom, the Netherlands, and France. The number of asylum seekers, real and bogus, began to decline after 2002, following the introduction of more stringent screening measures. The ethnic composition of the immigrants also changed; more recently the majority have come from Eastern Europe and the former Soviet Union, from Afghanistan and Chechnya.

This, very briefly, was the historical background of the emergence of Muslim communities.

The 2006 figures for Muslim communities in Europe are as follows (m = million):

France: about 5.5 m (having doubled since 1980)
Germany: 3.6 m (was 6,800 in 1961)
Britain: 1.6 m
Netherlands: 1.0 m (having more than doubled since 1980)
Sweden: 0.4 m (having tripled since 1980)
Denmark: 0.3 m (25,000 in 1982)
Italy: 0.9 m (120,000 in 1982)
Spain: 1.0 m (120,000 in 1982)
Greece: 0.5 m
Belgium: 0.5 m
Austria: 0.4 m (80,000 in 1982)

About 15 to 18 million Muslims in the Russian Federation should be added, as well as those making their home in Bosnia and Albania.

All of these figures are estimates; in a few cases they might be too high. According to some estimates, the number of Muslims in France could be as low as 3.5 to 4 million (5 million was the estimate of the French Ministry of the Interior for the year 2000). But most figures are certainly too low: The number of Muslims in Spain (which has the highest immigration rate in Europe) is perhaps closer to 1.5 million, and in Italy there are thought to be between 1 and 1.5 million, perhaps half of whom are illegal immigrants.

To what extent is it accurate to speak in terms of Muslim "communities," since they come from different parts of the world? Turkey is the country of origin of the great majority of Muslims living in Germany, and Turkish Muslims constitute 50 percent of those living in Austria and Greece, 40 percent of those in the Netherlands, and almost as large a percent in Belgium. But among these Turks there are hundreds of thousands of Kurds who, to put it cautiously, are not on the closest of terms with the Turks.

Most of the French and Spanish Muslims are of North African origin, as well as half of those in Italy and Belgium and perhaps 40 percent in the Netherlands. There has been considerable, mostly illegal, Muslim immigration from Albania into Italy. A sizable proportion of the illegal immigrants have continued to move to the north, but it is impossible to say how many have done so. British Muslims come from Pakistan (45 percent) and Bangladesh (15 percent or more).

Thus the communities in Europe are anything but monolithic. Except for in France they have no common language; few of them have a command of Arabic. But even though their number is relatively small, their political influence is growing. Thus the Muslim Association of Britain (MAB) is thought to be Arab-dominated. The great majority is Sunni, but there are also Shiite congregations (among Turks in Germany), Alawites (especially in Germany), Ahmadiya, considered beyond the pale by mainstream Muslims, and a variety of mystical (mainly Sufi) orders and groups.

Religion is very important in the life of the Muslim communities; the number of mosques in France has grown from about 260 in the mid-1980s to 2,000 or more at the present time. There are a few great mosques in cities such as Paris, Marseille, and Lyon; most are small, and the same is true with regard to Germany and other European countries. Germany had some 700 little mosques or prayer rooms in the 1980s, but there are more than 2,500 at the present time. There were 584 "certified mosques" in Britain in 1999, but the real number is at least 2,000 at present; in Birmingham, England's second largest city, there are more mosques now than churches, albeit much smaller ones. In West Ham, in eastern London, next door to the 2012 Olympic site, a mega mosque is planned to accommodate 70,000 worshipers. It could well be that there are now more practicing Muslims in Britain than members of the Church of England.

How orthodox are European Muslims? Estimates vary considerably. Mosque attendance on Friday prayers is thought to be as high as 60 percent in some places and as low as 10 percent in others, with the older generation, as usual, more frequently represented. A majority of young Muslims, born in Britain, do not understand the sermons given in languages such as Urdu, Bengali, and Arabic. Pilgrimage to Mecca (the haj), one of the pillars of Islam, is organized by Muslim organizations, but attendance is not very high—thought to be between 20,000 and 24,000 annually in Britain, 16,000 to 17,000 in Germany, and not much higher proportionally in other places. Given the fact that the fares are subsidized, these are not high figures.

In a poll among Turks living in Germany, 7 percent made it known that they were very orthodox, whereas 27 percent said that they were not very religious or not religious at all. (But other polls produced very different results; the figures were much higher for orthodox believers; much depends on the definition of "religious.") The length of their stay in Europe seems not to be of much relevance in this context, whereas education and income are of significance; those with higher education and higher income tend to be less religious than the rest. In a recent survey in France 36 percent said that they were strictly observant, but a far larger percentage obeyed individual commandments, such as observing the Ramadan fast. Some mosques are more orthodox than others; a certain proportion has the reputation of being the most "militant" (i.e., a reservoir for the recruitment of terrorists). This refers for instance to the mosques at Finsbury Park and Brixton in London, but these are not necessarily the most religiously orthodox. The religious orientation depends more on the personality of the imam (preacher). Recruitment and training of the militants is carried out in a variety of organizations in the general orbit of the mosques. Many mosques constitute something like an archipelago,

THE LAST DAYS OF EUROPE

with a variety of social organizations such as sport clubs (for men) and schools, kindergarten, and other institutions. The more mono-lithic the communities (such as in Germany) the more likely the emergence of a self-sufficient alternative society or subculture, and the less the need to learn the language of the country.

Muslim immigrants are not evenly distributed over the various European countries. The main concentrations are in the big cities and the old industrial regions. In the United Kingdom they are found in London (and within London they tend to settle in certain boroughs, such as Tower Hamlets in the East End) as well as in the Midlands (towns such as Bradford, Burnley, Oldham) but also Birmingham. In Germany, Berlin has the biggest Muslim community, but percentagewise they are even more strongly represented in the Ruhr/Rhein area (Essen, Dortmund, Duisburg, Solingen), and many other cities have a non-German population of between 25 and 30 percent, closely followed by Cologne. In France the strongest concentration is in the *banlieues,* the outer suburbs of Paris (such as Seine/Saint-Denis), with strong concentrations in southern France such as Toulouse, Lyon, Nice, and Côte d'Azur. But they are also found in the old industrial cities in northern France; many of the inhabitants of the Lille conurbation are Muslim. In Spain the main concentrations are in southern Spain and Madrid but also in Catalonia. In Sweden, Malmö, with such quarters as Rosengard, is the most Muslim city in Scandinavia by far, but there are also many Muslims in north and northwest Stockholm, in areas such as Tensta, and in eastern Göteborg. The influence of the antisecular Muslim Brotherhood has been particularly strong among the Islamic community in Sweden following the influx of radical anti-Western Saudi preachers.

Another peculiarity of the Muslim communities is the fact that they are considerably younger than the non-Muslim population. About half of the Muslims in Western and Central Europe were born there. While Muslims constitute only about 15 percent of the population of Brussels, they are 25 percent or more of the cohort of those under twenty-five—and, as noted earlier, more than 55 percent of the children born were of immigrant parents. The respective percentages in the major Dutch cities are higher. According to projections, the population of foreigners (most of them Muslim) in the year 2015 will be more than 40 percent in West German cities such as Cologne, Düsseldorf, Wuppertal, Duisburg, and many others. Altogether, the number of Muslims in Germany will double during the next decade while the native German population will decrease.

The problem facing West European societies is more often than not the second- and third-generation young immigrants—the very people who it was expected would be well integrated, equal members of these societies but who, on the contrary, revolted against their country of adoption. The reasons usually given are poverty (two-thirds of British Muslims live in low-income households), inadequate housing and overcrowding, ghettoization, unemployment, especially of the young, lack of education, racial prejudice on the part of their non-Muslim neighbors—all of which are said to lead to a lack of social mobility, crime, and general marginalization of the Muslim communities. By implication or directly, it is argued that it is the fault of the state and of society that these and other misfortunes have taken place. However, Muslims who have had successful careers in business or the professions say almost without exception that their ethnic identity did in no way hamper them.

To what extent has ghettoization been enforced by the outside world, and to what degree was it self-imposed? That new immigrants congregate in certain parts of a city is a well-known phenomenon. It can be studied, for instance, in London, where, traditionally, Irish (Camden Town), Jews (East End and later Golders Green), Australians and Poles (near Earls Court and Olympia), blacks (Brixton), Japanese (South Hampstead), and other newcomers settled at first. They were motivated by the wish to be among people who spoke their language and have ethnic food shops, travel agencies, clubs, and other organizations. The Russian immigrants to Berlin in the 1920s congregated in Charlottenburg, while poor Jews from Eastern Europe settled in the eastern part of the city.

A similar process took place as far as the Muslim immigration was concerned, but there was a basic difference: Earlier immigration waves did not receive any help with their housing on the part of the state or the local authorities, whereas in the second half of the twentieth century such assistance was the rule rather than the exception. For this reason there was little incentive to move out from lodgings that, however inadequate or displeasing, were free or inexpensive. When Eastern European Jews first moved to Whitechapel toward the end of the nineteenth century and the beginning of the twentieth, there was no mayor of London who went out of his way to help them. They and other immigrants had to fend for themselves, facing incomparably greater difficulties—for instance, there was no health service or other social assistance—than present-day immigrants. Muslim newcomers apparently like to stick longer with their coreligionists than do other groups of immigrants, and they are encouraged by their preachers to do so. This is true even with regard to India, where there is more ghettoization than in Europe; even middle-class Muslims seem to be reluctant to leave the areas where members of their community live.

The sites around Paris where many of the French Muslim

immigrants live and which exploded in November 2005 were un-comfortable and aesthetically displeasing, but they were not slums like London's East End. Yet it was precisely in these quarters that, in the words of a foreign visitor, an antisociety grew up infused with a burning hatred of the other France and deep distrust and alienation (see the online article "The Barbarians at the Gates of Paris" by Theodore Dalrymple). This hatred, in Dalrymple's words, manifests itself in the desire to scar everything around them—inscribing graffiti and torching motorcars. Benevolence inflames the anger of the young men. Although they enjoy a far higher stan-dard of living or consumption than they would in the country of their parents, this is no cause for gratitude; on the contrary, it is felt as an insult or a wound, even as they take it for granted as their due. "Barbarians" seemed a harsh, perhaps even racist, term, but was it wholly unjustified? One of the major gangs in the *banlieues* that had been involved in various criminal-terrorist activities (such as the abduction and murder of Ilan Halimi in January 2006) proudly called itself the Barbarians.

Housing has been mentioned as perhaps the main reason for the Paris riots of 2005, youth unemployment as another. Unem-ployment amounts to 30 to 40 percent in France and Germany and not much less in Britain and the Netherlands. As a Berlin head teacher put it, "We are creating an army of long-term unem-ployed." The rate of dropouts is very high among Turkish youth in Berlin and also in other European countries; it is much higher among boys than among girls. Only 3 percent of Muslim youth make it to college in Germany. Their language skills are low, which is not surprising because Turkish or Arabic is spoken at home, books are not found in many households, and the use of German (or English) is discouraged by the parents, who often do not master the language. Boys are sent to Koran schools but are not encouraged to study other subjects. Girls are often forbidden to go to school beyond the age of sixteen, let alone attend universities, because there they might be exposed to undesirable influences. When a Berlin school decided (after consultation with students and their parents) to insist on the use of the German language only at school, it came under heavy attack by the Turkish media even though most pupils and their parents favored the measure. Some well-meaning local protagonists of multiculturalism joined the protest because they believed that this was tantamount to cultural repression. But can a young generation advance socially and culturally unless they have mastered the language of the land?

Racism and xenophobia have been identified as factors responsible for the underachievement of Muslim youth. But this explanation fails to account for the scholastic success of pupils with an Indian and Far Eastern background, who score higher in most subjects than the average German or British student. Nor does it explain why Muslim girls acquit themselves much better than the boys. Could it be connected with the fact that girls are not allowed to go out in the street unaccompanied, whereas the boys spend most of their time there? Indian pupils in British schools have been doing twice as well as the Pakistanis, and those from the Far East have been outpacing almost everyone else.

There are many explanations, but the idea sometimes voiced that it is all the fault of the state or society is not plausible and will not help remedy the situation. Young people are told day in, day out, that they are victims of society and that it is not really their fault if they fail. As a result of these failures, a youth culture of violence and crime has developed that has little to do with religion. Despite attendance at Koran schools (more in Germany, with higher attendance, than in France and the United Kingdom), these young men are not well versed in their religion. They may go to the mosque on Fridays but will drink and take drugs afterward despite the religious ban. The main influence on these young people is neither the parental home nor the imams but the street gang. The parents have little authority, their way of life does not appeal to the offspring, they are not assertive enough, and they work too hard and earn too little. Old-fashioned Islam is of no great interest to many of them, either; a well-positioned imam in Britain said that "we are losing half of them." Only a few charismatic religious leaders who preach extreme action may have a certain following among young males. To understand the scenes in the schools and streets of Kreuzberg and the *banlieues,* a textbook on juvenile delinquency could be more helpful than the Koran.

School has the least authority; in France and the United Kingdom language is less of an impediment, but in Germany the pupils quite literally often do not understand what the teacher is saying and there is no effort to understand either the teacher or fellow pupils from other countries with different native languages. Many teachers do not succeed in imposing their authority, for if they dare to punish pupils for misbehavior or make any demands on them, they are accused of racism and discrimination. The streetwise pupils are adept at playing the race card.

Muslim youth culture varies to a certain extent from country to country. Common to them is the street sports gear (hooded sweatshirts, sneakers, etc.) and the machismo; their body language expresses aggression. They want respect, though it is not clear how they think such respect has been earned; perhaps it is based on the belief that "this street (quarter) is ours." In France and the United Kingdom hip-hop culture plays a central role; the texts of their songs express strong violence, often sadism. The street gang usually has a territorial base; Turks in Berlin have their own gangs, and the same is true with regard to Arabs and Kurds who arrived later in Germany. Sometimes the street gang is based on a certain village or district in the old country where the (extended) family originated. There has been a great deal of fighting between these territorial gangs; in Britain it has been quite often blacks against Indians (or Pakistanis) or, as in Brussels, Turks against black Africans.

Street gangs linger about aimlessly and often engage in petty crime. In Britain gangs of Muslim background have largely replaced the Afro-Caribbeans as drug pushers, though the key positions are usually not in their hands. Dealing in stolen goods is another way to earn the money needed for their gear, hashish (heavier drugs are sold but seldom consumed), and other entertainment. Teachers do not dare to interfere, and the local police are reluctant to make arrests, for judges will usually release those who have been arrested, especially if they are underage. Some proceed to more serious forms of crime. This is a theme that the European Muslim communities have been very reluctant to deal with. Crime figures are difficult to obtain, but all experts agree that the percentage of young Muslims in European prisons far exceeds their proportion in the population. This also goes for cases of rape, which in many gangs have become part of the rite of passage, especially in France, and to a lesser degree in the United Kingdom, Scandinavia, and Australia. The victims are by no means always non-Muslim girls or women who "asked for it" through immodest attire and behavior but also sometimes young Muslim women; the *hijab* does not by any means always offer protection.

Once upon a time the United States had the reputation of being a violent, crime-ridden country, in contrast to peaceful Europe. But in recent years European crime rates have converged with U.S. rates and in some respects have overtaken them, as Gerald Alexander has shown in an interesting study ("The Continent of

Broken Windows," *The Weekly Standard,* November 21, 2005). More assaults are committed in the United Kingdom than in the United States, while Swedes, Norwegians, and Dutch have roughly the same rates. Theft is higher in Britain, Denmark, France, Germany, and Norway (the Copenhagen theft rate is five times that of New York City). Burglary and robbery are as common in the United Kingdom, the Netherlands, the Scandinavian countries, and Germany as in the United States. (There has been very recently a slight decline in a few European countries such as Germany, but this has not affected the general trend.) The homicide rate is still higher in the United States than in Europe, but the American rate has declined, whereas there has been a significant increase in Europe. This rise in European crime cannot, of course, be attributed only to immigration, but there is no doubt that it is one of the main reasons. The head of the London Metropolitan Police made it known that 80 percent of the crime committed on the London Underground was carried out by immigrants from Africa. The head of Berlin's police announced that one out of three young immigrants in that city had a criminal record. Such statistics mentioning ethnic or religious background are forbidden in France, but the high number of young Muslims in French prisons (70 percent of the prison population according to some estimates) is no secret.

How does one account for the great aggressiveness of these gangs, as manifested, for instance, in the French riots of November 2005 but also on many occasions before and after? Their lack of achievement undoubtedly adds to the general discontent. The issue of identity (or lack of it) is frequently mentioned in this context. Many of the young (second) generation do not feel at home in either the parents' homeland or the country in which they live. They feel that they are not accepted in Europe and may curse the host country in all languages, but they would feel even less at home in Turkey or North Africa or on the Indian subcontinent, and they have no wish to return to these homelands. As mentioned earlier, when Algeria plays France in soccer they will root for Algeria, but mainly as a manifestation of protest and to annoy the French, rather than out of a sense of deep identification with the home of their parents or grandparents.

Sexual repression almost certainly is another factor that is seldom, if ever, discussed within their communities or by outside observers. It could well be that such repression (as Tsvetan Todorov has explained) generates extra aggression, an observation that has also been made by young Muslim women. Young Muslim men cannot freely meet members of the opposite sex from inside their own community; homosexuality is considered an abomination, yet in fact according to many accounts it is frequently practiced—as it has been all through Muslim history. The rejection of the other society manifests itself in many ways, beginning with defacing of walls of buildings and escalating to the torching of cars, as has happened frequently in France. In extreme cases there is an urge to destroy everything at hand and to attack all comers, including the firefighters and first-aid technicans rushing to the ghettos to deal with an emergency.

Socioeconomic factors have been blamed, and in this respect there have been interesting similarities to young black males in the United States: If only more jobs would be offered, it is often maintained, everything would change for the better. But many studies have shown that when such jobs were offered (as in the Clinton years in the United States), the takers were predominantly immigrants from Latin America and the Far East. There is enormous reluctance (as Orlando Patterson of Harvard has observed) to accept cultural explanations for the plight of young blacks. (There was also the interesting fact that all these findings did not apply to black

girls.) "Why were the young males flunking out?" The candid answer was what the sociologists call cool-pose culture, which was
too gratifying to give up. For these young men it was almost like a
drug, hanging out on the streets after school, shopping and dress-
ing sharply, enjoying sexual conquests and party drugs and hip-
hop music and culture. They found this subculture immensely
fulfilling, and it also brought them a great deal of respect from
white youth. It was not clear, however, why unemployment should
more or less automatically lead to a life of crime and drugs; there is
high unemployment in Pakistan and India, in North Africa and
Latin America, but much less crime and drugs.

These general observations apply to a large degree to Muslim
communities all over Europe, but there are also significant differences between them, their ethnic origins, and the way these communities came into being and developed over time. It is to these
specific aspects that we have to turn next.

France: Algeria to Paris

FRANCE IS HOME to the largest Muslim community in Europe,
which is largely the heritage of French colonial rule in North
Africa. Most French Muslims hail from Algeria and Morocco.
Since the French state does not count religious and ethnic data,
their number remains unknown; estimates vary greatly, between
3.5 and 6 million. About one-third live in the Greater Paris area,
another third between Marseille and Nice, and there are also massive concentrations in the industrial north, such as the Lille-
Roubaix-Tourcoing area. The birthrate of women from North

Africa was 5 percent in the 1970s; it has since declined to 3.5 percent but is still twice as high as the French birthrate. In cities such as Lille and Roubaix more than half of the young generation is Muslim by origin. About half of the French Muslims are French citizens by birth or naturalization.

French policy toward its Muslims has been based on the principles of secularism *(laïcité),* following the division between church and state established by law in 1905, and assimilation. There is the French republican belief in a homogeneous society; multiculturalism is rejected.

But the French model has not worked very well, even though other models in Europe have not worked much better. For a long time it was believed that riots, plundering, and gang warfare (as in Lyon in 1990 and other places in southern France and in Strassbourg and Lille) were local spontaneous affairs, which indeed they may have been. It was thought that given time and help, above all financial aid by state and local authorities, such events would not recur. There was a wave of terrorism, mainly in northern France and Paris, that peaked in 1994–95 but soon blew over. The violence, which was sparked to some degree by the situation in the Middle East and in particular in Algeria, was restricted to relatively small groups of youth, and the harsh but efficient action of French security forces put an end to it.

By and large it was believed that the situation among the immigrant communities was under control. But there were early warnings by those familiar with the situation in these quarters that tensions were rising and that the second- and third-generation *beurs* (or *beurettes*), the offspring of the original immigrants, were becoming more and more radicalized. A culture of violence and destruction prevailed that manifested itself, for instance, in torching cars (45,000 in 2005) and in gang warfare in general. It was not just a case of rejecting France and its values but of *hating* French society and its institutions, as spokesmen of the young generation repeatedly declared. By the year 2000, nearly a thousand "no-go" zones for the police had emerged in the immigrant quarters— unless of course the security officers appeared in force. At the same time it was estimated that more than half of the inmates of French prisons were of Muslim origin. This radicalization, which reached its climax in the riots of November 2005, was not primarily religious in character. True, there had been a process of Islamization among the community, but it is doubtful whether the young generation was mainly motivated by religious orthodoxy or piety. If girls opted for the *hijab,* as many but not most of them did, it was an act of defiance (or submission) more than the fulfillment of a religious duty.

Various reasons for the violence have been suggested, such as the resentment of *beurs* for not being accepted as full-fledged French, other instances of discrimination, and of course youth unemployment and other social problems. When François Mitterrand was president he described eloquently the hopelessness of this lost generation in these poor suburbs. But neither Mitterrand nor his party had a solution for these social ills or a way to give fresh hope to this generation. And it is an open question whether the problem could have been solved by administrative means. Something was missing in this generation—something that had not been missing in earlier immigration communities such as those of the Poles, the North African Jews, or the Chinese in Paris's thirteenth arrondissement or the Vietnamese who had settled in France. These groups had done surprisingly well; their motivation to get an education and to rise on the social ladder must have been different. True, these had been much smaller groups of immigrants, but unlike the North Africans they had received no help from the authorities. If there should be more xenophobia now, it could well be due in part to the reaction of the white working class against the preferential treatment that was frequently given to the new immigrants.

The racism of French (or German or British) society is frequently identified as the main reason for tensions and conflict between immigrant groups and their new home. The existence of racial prejudice and ethnic tensions all over the world is, unfortunately, an undisputed fact; it would be difficult to think of a single country in the first, second, or third world that is altogether free of it. But it is by no means obvious that racism is stronger now than it was fifty or a hundred years ago. While new immigrants may face prejudice in the job market and in many other fields, this has not prevented their integration in past ages. Russian immigrants in France faced similar difficulties in the 1920s and '30s, but this did not prevent their gradual integration and social rise. Why should a different situation prevail now? This question is only seldom asked, but without looking for root causes, strategies to ameliorate the situation will not be found.

There have been more than a few success stories among the North Africans, people who succeeded in many fields of achievement, who worked their way into the middle class and moved out of the ghettos. It has been mentioned earlier that whereas many male youths complained about discrimination (e.g., "What chances do I have with my name and address?"), few females had similar complaints: Their names and addresses were not an insurmountable obstacle. But the successful were still a minority. There must have been something in the mental makeup of those who felt themselves marginalized that made it difficult for them to succeed in life.

Successive French governments have tried without much

success to influence developments within the Muslim community. Of the many hundreds of imams, only 4 percent had French nationality, many of the others did not know French or had imperfect command of the language, and dozens saw their main assignment as open incitement against the authorities. The French government, on the one hand, had the worst offenders deported and, on the other hand, offered financial help for the building of mosques, which in the past had been financed by Saudi Arabia and other foreign governments.

But the authorities found no partner on the other side. There were many groups but no central organization representing the Muslims in France. To that end, following a government initiative, the French Council for the Muslim Faith (Conseil français du culte Musulman, or CFCM) was founded in 2002, consisting of various central and regional Muslim groups. But it proved to be a source of disappointment to the government because unending debates led to no decision and no action. Eventually, in 2005, the French government established yet another central organization for the construction and maintenance of mosques, the training of preachers and teachers of religion, and other such purposes. It remains to be seen whether this new organization will prove more effective than the CFCM.

The most influential Muslim organization in France for the last two decades has been the Union des Organisations Islamiques de France (UOIF), whose orientation, broadly speaking, is that of the Muslim Brotherhood (which is banned in most Arab countries). Officially UOIF has no connection with the Muslim Brotherhood and other forms of extremism but, according to its charter, "works to help answer the religious, cultural, social and humanitarian needs of the Muslims in France. It participates in building individual and collective awareness toward a responsible and positive integration."

In reality, UOIF is a political organization closely connected with Sheikh Qaradawi, the influential television preacher of the Al Jazeera television network who is also head of the European Council for Fatwa and Research, a Muslim Brotherhood front organization that was once based in Britain but is now in Dublin. Qaradawi was declared persona non grata in the United States when his ties with the Al Taqwa Bank, an institution that belonged to the Al Qaeda and Hamas archipelago of front organizations, were discovered. Qaradawi and his French followers have claimed to be champions of women's rights in Islam, but he has also endorsed suicide bombings, calls for jihad, and anti-Jewish propaganda. At the same time, in order to prevent conflict with the authorities, UOIF and allied groups have declared that they condemn anti-Semitism and "reject the import, in the name of Islam, of foreign conflicts onto French territory." While not a terrorist organization, UOIF engages mainly in political propaganda preaching a fairly radical version of Islam.

The Fédération Nationale des Musulmans de France (FNMF) is somewhat more moderate; it is (or was) supported by the Moroccan government. In addition, there are two Turkish and a few African Muslim organizations, and the position of the Paris Grand Mosque, built in the 1920s and now headed by Dalil Boubakeir, is also preeminent because of the privilege of issuing halal certificates ("seals of approval" issued by a religious authority confirming that food is permissible according to Islamic law).

All these organization are small or very small; altogether they are associations of notables with perhaps no more than 10 to 20 percent of French Muslims. However, they have gained legitimacy and influence as the result of the French government's eagerness to regard them as their main partner among the Muslims. The original intention of the French initiative was to strengthen a more liberal, European version of Islam, but these organizations' effect has been to strengthen the more conservative and even radical forces among the notables. At the same time it was quite uncertain whether and to what extent (as in the United Kingdom) these notables have much real influence on the younger generation in their midst.

How religious are French Muslims? According to a 2001 poll, 36 percent regard themselves as observant believers, but only 20 percent attend prayers at a mosque on Fridays and only 33 percent pray daily. However, 70 percent keep the Ramadan fast. A comparison with a similar poll in 1994 shows an increase of 10 to 20 percent, and it also appears that the Algerians, the most politicized, are the least observant as far as religious practice is concerned. (About 35 percent of France's Muslims come from Algeria, 25 percent from Morocco, and the rest from Tunisia and sub-Saharan Africa.)

The integration of Muslims in France did not work well. There were early manifestations of discontentment (and worse), but they were usually of a local character. Much (but by no means all) of the Muslim ire was directed against Jews. The molestation of Jewish pupils in schools was frequent, and these incidents could only be solved by a division between the ethnic groups. However, politicization was by no means total. A leading socialist candidate, Dominique Strauss-Kahn, was elected in Sarcelles, a predominantly North African city near Paris that also contained many Jews, and the candidate running against him was also Jewish. But with all this, Sarcelles, a city of some sixty thousand inhabitants, is as good a place as any to study the prevailing tensions, with the Jews living in the center and the Muslims in the more distant quarters, with hardly any common meeting points.

The situation deteriorated when the issue of the *hijab* arose. Around 1989 in the wake of the Islamization wave it became the fashion among some girls, usually under parental guidance, to attend school with the well-known head scarf. But wearing the *hijab* was in stark contradiction to French law and tradition, which banned ostentatious display of religious symbols in schools. Furthermore, it was not clear whether wearing the *hijab* was indeed a religious or a political statement. The great majority of French teachers and the public in general opposed the practice as illegal. There was also the question of the protection of the Muslim girls from secular families—many, perhaps the majority, had no wish to jump on the Islamist bandwagon.

This dispute continued for more than a decade. Some of the leading Muslim dignitaries announced that wearing the *hijab* in school, while desirable, was not a religious obligation, but the more extreme elements insisted on it. The problem could have been solved by sending those who wanted the *hijab* at any price to Muslim schools, but there was no great enthusiasm for this solution, either. The case was brought to court, and courts took different decisions.

Far more ominous were the riots that started on October 28, 2005, in Clichy-sous-Bois, an eastern suburb of Paris, when a police patrol arrived to check identity papers and two youngsters who had been playing soccer ran away, landed in a high-power electricity facility, and were electrocuted. There were several versions about the reason for their running away without being chased—but the rumor that they had been killed by the police quickly spread and in the following nights gangs roamed the area destroying property, pillaging and burning schools, day-care centers, youth clubs, and other institutions, attacking police and firefighters. The most frequent targets were cars; while the torching of cars and trucks had been customary even in quieter days, the number rose to hundreds during the riots.

These riots spread within a few days to other parts of France and in a very few cases also outside France. Altogether some 274 communes were affected, about nine thousand cars were burned in twenty days of rioting, and twenty-eight hundred arrests were made. No one was killed in the attacks, but hundreds were injured both among the police and the attackers. The material damage was estimated at more than 200 million euros. On November 8 President Chirac announced a state of emergency and police reserves were brought in. On November 17 Chirac announced a return to normal conditions, since in the previous night only close to a hundred cars had been burned.

These events caused consternation and even shock in France and the rest of the world. The French authorities had believed that despite all setbacks the French model was working and could serve as an example to other European countries. During the first days of the riots the leading personalities of the republic preferred not to comment; the only one who did was Nicolas Sarkozy, the minister of the interior, who was bitterly attacked by the rioters and their well-wishers because he compared them to vermin that had to be removed. Sarkozy, however, known for plain speaking, had been the main advocate of positive discrimination on behalf of the minorities, and his views and comments were shared by most French people. ("Positive discrimination" is a policy similar to what is called affirmative action in the United States.)

Who were the rioters and what were their motives? The reasons given were the usual: unemployment, poverty, bad housing conditions, and racism on the part of the police and French society in general. All this no doubt played a role, but it could not provide a satisfactory answer. Nor does it appear that militant Islamism played a significant role; in fact, one of the Muslim organizations at one stage published a religious fatwa against the riots and toward the end of the riots, when the impetus was already fading, the "big brothers," the mosque militants, appeared in the street trying to restrain the attackers. Other Muslim organizations denounced the fatwa because, as they argued, the attacks had nothing to do with them. Unemployment was high (up to 45 percent) in the places in which rioting was most intense, but there were many neighborhoods with equally high unemployment rates in which there was no unrest.

All of the rioters were young—many very young, aged twelve or thirteen—which posed a problem for police and judges who could not detain people underage. Except for some Portuguese, the rioters were mostly of North or black African origin and belonged to street gangs that were not religiously motivated. In other times and conditions, they would have followed a leader of either the extreme right or the extreme left.

In places in which drug dealing was endemic, few, if any, attacks occurred, because the drug dealers did not want their business to be affected. Generally speaking, it remains to be explored why riots occurred in certain parts of France but not in others (e.g., Marseille, Bordeaux). Was it that living conditions in Paris were particularly bad? Was it because the rioters were better organized in the Paris *banlieues*? There seems to be general agreement that the riots were spontaneous and that there was no hidden hand organizing and coordinating the attacks. But it was also believed that similar major outbursts might happen again and that they could occur not only in France. Historians of nineteenth-century Paris pointed to the emergence of "dangerous classes" prone to engage in violence, individual crime as well as collective action, and it seemed that a similar phenomenon had recurred.

What lessons were drawn by the French government?

There was of course much eagerness to defuse the tensions

by creating new jobs, but this was bound to be difficult at a time when unemployment was already high in France. There have been many schemes to this end over the past decades without, however, significant success. Interior Minister Nicolas Sarkozy has suggested that 15 percent of all places in French higher education should be reserved for these minorities.

Such measures of positive discrimination may not be easy to carry out in France with its taboos on identifying the ethnic and religious backgrounds of individuals. These traditions may have to be shed, along with the resistance to according preferential treatment to people on the basis of race or religion. A policy of "equal opportunities" will replace the old policy of integration. It will have to be tried, but there is no certainty that it will work. It is not known, after all, how eager the young unemployed are to accept work or the extent to which they would be capable of succeeding in the French educational system even if they are granted special conditions. It will be difficult for the government to assure employment to those who were given preferential treatment.

New organizations have been established, such as the High Authority for the Struggle Against Discrimination and for Equality (Haute autorité de lutte contre les discriminations et pour l'égalité, or HALDE) in answer to the complaints about racism. But racism in France has not been a one-sided affair; there has been a great deal of anti-French feeling, not to mention the attacks by immigrants against other minorities such as Jews. In fact, there has been little or no envy on the part of the French but, on the contrary, pride about the achievement of those North Africans who made it—such as Zinedine Zidane, the son of a very poor Berber family who grew up in the *banlieues* and became the most well-paid soccer player in the world, as well as the pride of French soccer.

Some French sociologists have argued that while social and

economic integration has largely failed, cultural assimilation has been quite successful, but this is probably true only concerning certain aspects of mass culture, which are shared by the majority and the minority. But it also seems true that certain habits persist in the Muslim communities that are repugnant to the majority of French; a figure of 70,000 forced marriages has been mentioned and 35,000 cases of female circumcision. These figures cannot be verified—they could be exaggerated or an understatement. There is a long way to go to true cultural integration.

Germany:
Eastern Anatolia to Berlin

THE NUMBER OF Muslim immigrants in Germany is about 3.5 million, of whom some 75 percent are of Turkish origin. About a third of them are concentrated in North Rhine-Westphalia, another third in Berlin. It is a much younger community than German society generally, and the birthrate is also far higher. The first young Turkish workers arrived in the late 1950s, hired by German enterprises suffering from an acute lack of manpower. It was assumed that they would come to Germany on a temporary basis, but in fact only a few returned at first, and later on, having been offered a certain sum of money in order to go back to Turkey, some fifty-five thousand of them did. In the 1970s the need for guest workers sharply declined. However, the young workers who had settled in Germany went back to their ancestral villages and returned to Germany with their brides or spouses. Immigration from Turkey continued in any case because German immigration practice was lax. If the newcomers claimed that they came as asylum seekers because they were being persecuted in their homelands (as in the case of the Kurds), they were accepted even if seeking political asylum was a secondary reason for their immigration. The prospects of a higher living standard were much greater in Germany, and if they did not find a job they received social assistance.

In no other country have immigrants been the subject of so many initiatives by so many well-intentioned institutions to promote their integration—social workers, academic researchers, churches eager to enter a dialogue, political parties (such as the Greens and the Liberals) interested in gaining a foothold in these communities. The social workers and the "migration experts" did some good work, such as protecting the new immigrants against exploitative landlords, but on balance probably did more harm than good. They showed the Turks how to work the social safety net—that is to say, to get a maximum of financial and other aid from the state and the local authorities with a minimum of contribution to the common good. What the Turkish community needed above all was advice and help in the field of *education,* which would have enabled them to advance on the social ladder. Instead, as even a brief walk through major German cities from Berlin to Cologne and Duisburg will show, a parallel society has emerged in Germany, and the problems facing German society today are the same as in France and Britain: ghettoization, re-Islamization, high youth unemployment, and failure in the educational system.

The Turkish (and Kurdish) immigrants were in no way prepared for life in Europe. They came from the least developed parts of Turkey such as Eastern Anatolia, many were illiterate, and they were far more conservative in both their religious beliefs and political orientation than middle-class Turkish society in Istanbul or Ankara. The newcomers knew no German—in contrast to many immigrants to France or Britain, who usually had at least a smattering of French or English. Thus it came as no surprise that almost from the moment of their arrival in Germany the Turks confined themselves to their own kind and customs: their own mosques, halal and vegetable shops, and various other places in which they could be among their fellow Turks.

They did not mind that their children went to German schools but bitterly opposed the idea that the girls should participate in sports, class excursions, or biology lessons in which there would be talk about sex. They opposed the teaching of subjects, however innocent, that could be construed as being not in conformity with their religion. They insisted on Islamic tuition in school and went to court to achieve their demand (which was not easily compatible with the German constitution). In the end they got their way. German authorities were paying for the teachers of religion, most of whom came from abroad, were fundamentalists, and knew little or no German.

There was no supervision of what kind of tuition (or indoctrination) took place in these lessons. True, German authorities have been insisting that religious tuition should be in German, but this has been strongly resisted by the Turkish religious organizations and also the Turkish government. German courts when in doubt took a pro-Muslim stand. The courts rejected the complaints of non-Muslim neighbors about the noise created by the mosques' loudspeakers amplifying the calls and prayers of the muezzin. Such decisions, however well intended, did not contribute to good relations between Muslim and non-Muslim neighbors.

Those Muslims who had settled in Germany felt that they were different from their German surroundings, which they rejected for religious and other reasons. Once they had established families, the urge to maintain their otherness became even stronger—to be like a German was immoral. No one thought to leave Germany in protest against the infidels—this, after all, was their little world and, God willing, might eventually be their own country. True, the younger generation, particularly the boys and young men, adopted the attire of their German contemporaries, but still very often the only book in their homes was the Koran.

In view of its reactionary social-cultural-religious orientation the Turkish community in Germany was of particular interest to the right-wing fundamentalist forces in Turkey headed by Necmittin Erbakan. His extremist party sent emissaries and imams to Germany and provided guidance in a variety of ways. The two principal organizations were Cemaleddin Kaplan's Khalifat group in Cologne and Milli Goerues, an association founded in the 1980s that spread quickly through Germany and, to a lesser extent, through the Turkish communities in other European countries. The Kaplan group remained relatively small; it rejected democracy as a matter of principle and saw its main enemy not so much in Germany but in secular Turkey. According to the teaching of the Turkish fundamentalists, the Jews had founded two states—Israel and Turkey—because the founders of modern Turkey, the Young Turks and Kemal Atatürk, had all been Doenme by origin, that is to say, Jews who centuries ago had converted to Islam with the intention gradually to subvert, modernize, and secularize it.

Kaplan died in 1995 and his son Metin Kaplan succeeded him as leader of the Khalifat group. Soon afterward their hero and sponsor Erbakan was elected prime minister of Turkey, but he was not reelected and was eventually banned from politics. These events in Turkey, which led to a split among the Turkish fundamentalists, with similar splits among their followers in Germany, are outside the scope of my narrative. Suffice it to say that Erbakan, a professor of physics who had lived in Germany for many years, was eventually succeeded by Recep Tayyip Erdoğan, once a semiprofessional soccer player, who became prime minister in 2003 after having served as a popular mayor of Istanbul. Erdogan, while essentially also a fundamentalist, moved more cautiously than his predecessor. He favored Turkey's entry into the European Community and improved relations with Greece, and in domestic politics he followed a conservative but more circumspect and pragmatic course.

In recent years the Turkish government has taken great interest in the Turkish communities in Germany, through official and unofficial channels. The great majority of Turks in Germany get their information about their own affairs and the world from Turkish newspapers such as *Hurriyet,* with editions printed in Berlin, as well as from Turkish television. Visitors to Kreuzberg or Moabit will find that hardly a single apartment is without a satellite dish on the balcony to facilitate reception of channels from the homeland. Even their sports news originates in a publication with the interesting title *Fanatik.* The notorious "ultrapatriotic" movie *Valley of the Wolves* had a tremendous success among the Turkish community in Germany and got standing ovations.

The Kaplan group by its very radicalism had largely isolated itself from the mainstream of German Turks; there was even political murder in an internal struggle for power. Eventually Metin Kaplan was sentenced to four years in prison for incitement to murder, and after serving this sentence he was deported to Turkey with his family. (He was wanted in Turkey because he had planned to crash a plane against the Atatürk mausoleum on the occasion of a celebration.) The city of Cologne tried meanwhile to retrieve more than 200,000 euros that had been paid to Metin Kaplan as social assistance; earlier on during a police raid more than a million dollars and much gold had been found in his apartment. This case of European authorities unknowingly subsidizing terrorist activities and police and courts being hampered by political or legal considerations from taking effective countermeasures was by no means an exceptional occurrence.

Kaplan's Khalifat group was eventually declared illegal. The followers, however, remained a sect, whereas Milli Goerues, acting more cleverly, became a mass organization. Milli Goerues has claimed all along that it respected the German constitution and believed in democracy, even subscribing to "European values." But German domestic intelligence (the agency responsible for the protection of the constitution) as well as many knowledgeable outside observers believed that the opposite was true even though the Turkish Islamists made great efforts to ingratiate themselves with the ruling Christian Democratic Union (CDU). The Milli Goerues vision is one of a country living according to strict Islamic law, even if certain concessions have to be made at present until the Muslims constitute a majority. They claim that their party is no more antidemocratic than the CDU. Until about twenty years ago the Turkish religious organizations were indeed neutral and the sermons in the mosques apolitical. But since then the leading groups, including DITIB (a branch of the Turkish ministry of religious affairs), have been taken over by Islamists, often radical Islamists. At the same time, these organizations have threatened legal action (and frequently taken it) against those revealing their true orientation and activities. "Milli Goerues" means "National Vision" and is also the title of a book by the Turkish extremist leader Erbakan. It claims to have some 220,000 members (the true figure seems to be closer to 20,000), and runs some 270 mosques in Germany.

In their ideological guidelines Milli Goerues and allied organizations are sharply critical of Christianity and are openly anti-Semitic. On occasion they have expressed sympathy with Muslim

terror groups, but as far as can be ascertained they have not partic-
ipated in such actions. Al Qaeda and other terrorist organizations
that have used Germany as a recruiting ground have as a rule concentrated on immigrants from Arab and North African communities.

While the aim of German policy has been the integration of
the Turkish communities, the aim of the Islamist organizations
supported by the Turkish government has been diametrically opposed to integration. The Turks in Germany remain Turks even if
they have adopted the German nationality; according to Ankara's
wishes, Turks in Germany should vote in Turkish elections and, at
the same time, wherever they live they should promote the interests
of Greater Turkey, which remains their fatherland. (Turks born in
Germany do not automatically acquire German citizenship but
may apply for it.) German official institutions have been quite helpless in these confrontations with the Islamists. Christian churches
have gone out of their way to look for a dialogue and commonali-
ties between the religions. They have not found any partners in this
endeavor, however, for the aim of the Turkish religious institutions
has been to preserve their separate character, not to be influenced
by Western religion, culture, or political values. This failure has not
been restricted to Germany; accounts from Austria and Switzerland report the same seemingly insoluble problems. Only in recent
years have the churches given up what was quite obviously a fruitless endeavor.

What have been the main points of contention between the
Islamists and the German society in which (or parallel to which)
they live? According to German officials, their number is not
formidable—3,600 in Berlin—and it has not grown significantly
over the years. But this refers to militants, professionals, or semi-
professionals, and seen from this perspective they are stronger than

any other group. Milli Goerues, which has been categorized by German officials as "extremist," has hundreds of groups based in its mosques. It aims (without mincing words) to replace the secular order in the country in which they live by an order based on the sharia, first in the regions in which Muslims are the majority, or a significant minority, and subsequently in the areas in which their space has expanded. Such a political orientation is incompatible with the democratic order.

Those who know these communities well report that so far Milli Goerues and the other Islamist groups have opted for social pressure rather than violent action. Seven "honor killings" in five months of women who chose to live a free life "like the Germans" were the actions of individuals rather than an organized campaign. The perpetrators escaped with lenient punishment. Reports from Kreuzberg, Wedding, and other quarters convey interesting examples of how this social pressure manifests itself: Young men stop people in the streets and tell them that if they are not Muslims they should leave the neighborhood. German children have been driven out of local playgrounds. In school there has been pressure on non-Muslims during Ramadan to fast; non-Muslim girls have been pressured to wear clothes similar to those of the Muslim girls or, at least, not indecent skirts or trousers or T-shirts. Parents of schoolchildren have been told that whatever instructions the school may give them, the mosque and its classes always have priority. According to these reports, Islamist activists have not interfered with drug dealing or football (soccer), knowing that they would face great difficulties confronting popular entertainment.

One of the main points of contention has been the position of women. According to orthodox Islamist tradition, women should not be educated beyond a certain level. They should stay home and bring up the children, and they should leave home only accompanied by a male member (even a younger brother) of the family. Many, probably most, young women are married off by their parents to young men whom they have never seen before— the so-called forced marriages. This has become a major political issue owing to the activities (and books) of a few female dissidents who have made this practice known. Some German "migration researchers" have argued that these accusations are at the very least exaggerated, because the motive is usually economic: Marriages are arranged in order to safeguard the economic well-being of the family. Whatever the motive, the researchers have not denied the existence of this practice but explained it as a deeply rooted ethnic peculiarity among Turks and Kurds. They also believe that the authorities should not interfere with such traditions.

By and large there has been less physical violence between Muslim and non-Muslim communities in Germany than in France and Britain, but there is a great deal of distrust between the communities. With high youth unemployment and the failure of many young Muslims in school, the result of lack of motivation and Islamist indoctrination, there is the potential for conflict. Two figures are of considerable relevance in this context: 40 percent of young people of non-German origin in Berlin do not even graduate from *Hauptschule,* the lower stream of the educational system and the refuge of those who have failed. One in three of young people of non-German origin come in conflict with the law in Berlin before reaching the age of eighteen. Although the 40 percent of those who fail to graduate are boys and girls, it appears, since, as mentioned earlier, girls are doing considerably better in school than boys, that this is predominantly a problem of young males rather than the young generation in general. Hence the potential for violence in Berlin and other cities. The attitude of some German political parties seeking to gain votes in these communities has been less than helpful. Trying to protect the immigrants against criticism from outside, these parties have opposed social and cultural integration and supported separatism and the survival of a parallel society.

United Kingdom:
Bangladesh to the East End

THE 1.6 MILLION Muslims in Britain, mainly from Pakistan and Bangladesh (with a sprinkling of Somalis, Arabs, and others), constitute about half of the postwar immigrant population in Britain. In this respect, as in some others, their situation differs from the state of affairs in other European countries in which Muslim immigrants are the dominant factor. Britain's Muslim population is concentrated in certain parts, including London, Birmingham, the West Midlands, West Yorkshire, and Lancashire. In a few towns such as Dewsbury, the Muslims' part of the population is about 30 percent. They have not been politically more active than other immigrant groups, but in view of the radical activities of some sectors in these communities they have been more in the public eye than others.

They originally came from a few districts in India and Pakistan, such as parts of Jammu and Kashmir, Punjab, and the North-West Frontier Province, as well as Sylhet in Bangladesh. This was also reflected in their religious orientation, which largely followed the Indian pattern; the prevailing sects are the Indian Barelvi and Deobandis, quite orthodox but not extremist in a political sense. Those originating in Bangladesh brought with them a version of Islam that was influenced by moderate Sufi elements and Hindu folk religion. But in Britain, under the influence of fundamentalist preachers from Saudi Arabia and other parts of the Arab world, religious radicalization ("Arabization") took place.

Individual terrorists operating in Britain and other countries emerged from these circles. A report by the British Home Office (Ministry of the Interior) investigated the sources of anger, alienation, and disillusionment among young Muslims. This report mentions the belief that British foreign policy applies a double standard (e.g., in Kashmir, Palestine, and Iraq), not acting in conformity with Muslim interests in these conflicts. Furthermore, there are complaints about xenophobia and Islamophobia, inasmuch as the (innocent) majority of Muslims have been blamed for the violent attacks of a few.

While this argument may not be wholly baseless, it is also true (as the report concedes) that Muslims are more likely than other faith groups to have lower professional qualifications (two-fifths have none), to be unemployed and economically inactive, and to be overrepresented in deprived areas. Unemployment among young Muslims is at least three times higher than among the general population. In comparison, the situation of immigrant groups such as Indians, Sikhs, Cypriots, and many others is much better—there have been no reports about higher-than-average unemployment among young Indians and none about educational problems. In this respect, as in many others, the situation in Britain resembles that in Germany, France, and other European countries. The Muslim minority is doing less well than others and complains more than others about discrimination.

It has also been frequently noted that while Muslims have been more vociferous about their exclusion from the political process, they are less likely than other religious or ethnic groups to participate in civic activities and least likely to volunteer. To some extent, the specific difficulties with Britain's Muslims are rooted in their social origins; like the Turkish immigrants in Germany, they hail from certain backward districts and villages in their home country and are poorly educated, very religious, and ill prepared for life in a secular society. This separateness is perpetuated by not mixing with the local population, only seldom marrying outside their community, and preferring to import spouses from the same districts and villages they hail from.

Other immigrant groups have also tried hard to maintain their specific character but, unlike the Muslims, have not suffered from the feeling of being an oppressed group, nor has there been so much resentment and hate. In other words, among other communities it is widely believed that it is possible to be Indian and British, or Sikh and British, whereas among Muslims there is widespread belief that their allegiance is to Islam; being British citizens and benefiting from British social services does not imply a civic obligation toward the country in which they live. Changes have taken place in this respect: Another report about Bangladeshis in the East End published in the 1990s notes that when they first came they were reluctant to accept government social assistance, believing that this was dishonorable and contrary to their religion. It was only when they began following the advice given by social workers that dependence on social assistance as a way of life became acceptable and eventually endemic.

Through the Race Relations Act of 1976 and a variety of other human rights laws, the British government provided safeguards concerning the sensibilities of the Muslim communities. According to a variety of polls, the majority of British Muslims admitted that they were better treated in the United Kingdom than in other European countries. There was, for instance, no total legal ban in Britain, in contrast to France and Germany, to wearing the *hijab* in school. However, there were many complaints by the British underclass that the new immigrants were in fact given preferential treatment for housing and other benefits.

London ("Londonistan") became the refuge of many extremists who had been sentenced to long prison terms or even death in their native countries in the Arab world. They found a refuge in Britain, and radical organizations banned in most Arab countries (such as the Muslim Brotherhood) could operate freely in the United Kingdom. Nevertheless, 26 percent of Muslims interviewed felt no loyalty toward Britain; 40 percent opted for introducing the laws of sharia in certain parts of Britain (February 2006); 13 percent justified terrorist attacks Al Qaeda style and 47 percent supported suicide attacks such as in Israel. The results of such public opinion polls were often inconsistent; according to a poll in February 2006, 91 percent expressed loyalty to Britain, but 16 to 20 percent felt some sympathy with the bombers of July 7, 2005, who had killed more than forty people in London, and according to yet another poll, attitudes toward non-Muslims are more negative in Britain than in any other European country. (But almost 50 percent of those interviewed argued that the authorities were not severe enough in suppressing the violent elements in their midst—a clear sign that there is polarization among the Muslim communities.) It could well be that these figures err on the side of understatement, because it is unlikely that all of those asked would give replies that might bring them in conflict with the authorities.

While immigrant communities all over the world tend to stick together, at least during the first and second generation, this is particularly strong among the Muslims. According to polls, very few Muslims have non-Muslim friends. This applies particularly to the very orthodox, obeying the commandment of their religion not to have close relations with infidels, the *kufr*. It applies much less to the educated middle class, which is, however, quite small.

The main political organizations among British Muslims are the Muslim Council of Britain (MCB), the Muslim Association of Britain (MAB), and the Islamic Society of Britain (ISB). The Muslim Association of Britain has connections with the Muslim Brotherhood and Hamas; it concentrates on the struggle against Israel and cooperates closely with left-wing parties such as the Trotskyite Socialist Workers Party (SWP). One of its patrons was Ken Livingstone, the mayor of London who staunchly defended Qaradawi, the influential television sheikh and a frequent honorary guest in London, against all criticism. Qaradawi also followed the ambiguous line taken by the Muslim Brotherhood on terrorism: They claim to oppose terrorism on some occasions yet defend it on others. During the affair of the Danish cartoons in early 2006 he took a particularly militant line, calling virtually for a holy war worldwide. Livingstone claimed that Qaradawi was a much maligned progressive voice of moderation.

The Muslim Council of Britain (MCB) has been competing with the MAB for influence in the Muslim community; its roots are in Pakistani Islamist sects, whereas among the MAB leadership the Arab element is stronger. One of the leaders of the MCB is Iqbal Sacranie, who in 1989, during the furor over the publication of Salman Rushdie's *Satanic Verses,* went on record declaring that death was too easy a punishment for Rushdie. Sacranie was subsequently knighted, and as a spokesman for moderate Islam Sir Iqbal became an adviser of Prime Minister Tony Blair. But Saudi (Wahabi) influence has also grown inside the MCB, and as a result the British Muslim Forum (BMF) was founded in 2005. The British Muslim Forum is mainly Pakistani rather than Arab in character, distances itself from the more radical Saudis, and claims to represent more mosques than the other organizations.

Various radical initiatives were launched by and among British Muslims, including the idea of having a parliament of their own

(Kalim Siddiqi) as a first step toward establishing a separatist Muslim state in Britain. Other militants declared that their struggle would not be over until the green (or black) flag of Islam was hoisted over 10 Downing Street, the residence of the prime minister. One Muslim spokesman claimed there were no-go zones and not even a cabinet minister had a right to enter them. The same circles among British Muslims took an extremist stand on various occasions, such as the burning of Salman Rushdie's novel *The Satanic Verses* in the late 1980s. They were firmly opposed to moderate religious groups considered dissident (such as the Ahmadiya) that had mosques of their own. However, these militants distanced themselves from the London terrorist attacks of July 2005. They wanted to remain a legal organization, if possible, receiving support from the government while not deviating from their radical principles.

Among the most radical organizations are Hizb al Tahrir and Al Murabitun, which were banned in almost all Middle Eastern and European countries but long tolerated in Britain. They have continued their activities since under various covers. (The Blair government tried to outlaw them but faced opposition on the part of legal circles and also the security services.) Hizb al Tahrir, which means "party of liberation," advocates the restoration of the Caliphate (Khalifat); it has not openly advocated violence, but its members have been involved in terrorists attacks in various other parts of the world. It has been described as racist and totalitarian by its critics within the Muslim community, but it has found supporters among some prominent members of the British Labour Party such as Clare Short, a former government minister. Certain British mosques, such as the one in Finsbury Park, London, served as recruiting grounds for terrorists; they were not closed but came under observation by the authorities.

The position of Muslims in Britain was different from that in other European countries, partly because they were not a majority among the immigrant population and also because, in contrast to the Muslims in France and Germany, they were not a homogeneous group; those from Pakistan, Bangladesh, the Arab world, and so on, had quite literally no common language but English. The central organizations that had been founded, such as the MCB and the MAB, were by no means recognized by all British Muslims, and while the government usually regarded these groups as partners for dialogue, their authority within their community was not great, least of all among the younger generation. Furthermore, their neighbors with whom they came in daily contact and with whom also tensions arose were as often as not non-Muslim immigrants such as Indians, West Indians, and Africans, rather than native British. The Muslims' conflicts were with these sectors of the population as much as with the white majority.

The attitude of the British authorities was traditionally one of benign neglect: As long as the radical Muslim organizations did not commit flagrant breaches of peace, they were left alone. This began to change after September 11, 2001, the terrorist attacks in Britain on July 7, 2005, and the planned attacks of August 2006. The British authorities took a more active interest in the radical preachers inciting to murder; most of them had lived on social security, as had their colleagues in France and Germany. Exposure by the media had an effect: A few were deported from Britain; one, Abu Hamza al-Mizri, was sentenced to a seven-year prison term in 2006. By and large, however, the authorities believed that there was no alternative to establishing close relations and a dialogue with these elements in the Muslim community who were believed (often incorrectly) to be at least relatively moderate, even though not much help seems to have been given by the moderates in the struggle against terrorism and the prevention of attacks. Even when facing open incitement to murder such as in the "war of civilizations" demonstrations of February 2006, the security forces preferred to err on the side of restraint rather than acting according to the law of the land and thus ignored open appeals to murder. Among the banners at the demonstrations: "Slay [or behead] those those who insult Islam," "Exterminate those who slander Islam," "Freedom go to hell," and "Europe, take some lessons from 9/11."

MUSLIM IMMIGRATION INTO OTHER EUROPEAN countries began later and was, in the case of Spain and Italy, largely illegal; those who went to Scandinavia came to a considerable extent as political asylum seekers or within the framework of "reunification of families." Those who went to Italy (about a million) came from North Africa and settled mainly in northern Italy, because economic conditions in southern Italy were worse. Those who went to Spain (a million or more) settled all over the country.

Italy and Spain frequently served as mere transit locations, since state support in the northern countries was more substantial. This was quite easy to accomplish, since the borders between European countries had been virtually abolished (see Schengen accord earlier). For years the main route for illegal immigrants from North Africa was to Spain first by way of Ceuta and Melilla, and the Spanish authorities did not create great difficulties. But as the stream of the illegals was swelling and as other European countries complained about Spanish laxness, the border with Morocco was more effectively watched and Italy, with its 7,600-kilometer coastline, became the main gateway for illegal immigrants. Italy registered an increase of almost 70 percent in the arrival of illegal immigrants in 2005 compared with the year before, and it was clear that only some of the illegal arrivals had been counted.

As in Germany and France, these new immigrants eventually congregated in certain regions—the Milan area in Italy, with at least a hundred thousand residents, as well as Varese and Cremona in the north but also the Turin region. Among the religious leaders, usually Islamists, there were Egyptians but also radical preachers from Senegal and other black African countries. Other concentrations of Muslim immigrants settled in southern Spain and Catalonia as well as in Malmö in Sweden, Brussels, and the main cities in the Netherlands.

These immigrants were on the whole well treated, and at first, in the 1970s and '80s, there were few tensions. The authorities did not deport illegal immigrants, and there were hardly any restrictions on immigration. As the numbers of the new immigrants grew, however, it became clear that, contrary to expectations, most of them had no wish to become integrated in society. They established parallel societies and many did not bother to learn the language of the land, yet they made full use of the social services offered, such as housing, unemployment payments, and free medical services, which caused difficulties for the host countries at a time of financial stringency.

It gradually appeared that the contribution of many of these newcomers was not what had been hoped for. True, some were willing to accept work that few Swedes or Dutch (or French or Germans) were willing to do. But at the same time the crime rate in these communities and their part in the drug trade and other asocial behavior was considerably higher than the national average.

Members of these communities, particularly of the second generation as their numbers were growing, began to assert themselves politically and in other ways. This manifested itself most obviously perhaps in aggressive behavior in the streets—a frequent complaint by local residents—as if they wanted to demonstrate that *they* were the new masters in the country. At the same time, they were complaining that they were discriminated against, not sufficient respect was paid to them, and their religious or national sensitivities were not sufficiently taken into account. An illustrative example is the dispute about *The Last Judgment* by Giovanni di Modena, in the Bologna cathedral. This depicted, on the basis of Dante's *Divine Comedy*, how a naked Muhammad and a demon next to him were thrown into hell. The Union of Italian Muslims, headed by one Adel Smith, complained to the Pope and other church dignitaries and demanded the removal of this fresco (an even greater offense than Rushdie's *Satanic Verses*), even though it was almost impossible to see the prophet's figure from the ground.

Whether the fresco had indeed offended Mr. Smith or any-one else is doubtful; it is more likely that this was used as a pretext to increase tensions between the communities, to show the Muslim communities that they were being persecuted and that they had to rally, presumably under the leadership of Mr. Smith. The facts that the disputed painting was over five hundred years old and that in many Muslim countries churches were not even permitted to be built was immaterial.

Similar demands were made in other countries. The wearing of the *hijab* and the burka were widely perceived by non-Muslims as a political demonstration intended to provoke non-Muslims, bombs were thrown in Madrid, Theo van Gogh was killed in Am-sterdam, and in Denmark in late 2005 some members of the Mus-lim minority, offended by cartoon depictions of the Prophet Muhammad in a provincial newspaper, instigated a worldwide campaign that resulted in many dead and great political and eco-nomic damage to the country that had given them asylum.

To a large extent the Nordic countries, Belgium, and Holland had only themselves to blame. They had taken in immigrants in the belief that they had been persecuted in their homeland and that it was an elementary humanitarian duty to provide shelter, food, and other help to these unfortunate people. The host nations had, in the case of Norway and other countries, given asylum to terrorists wanted for murder in their own country. Asylum was given apparently in the sincere belief that these immigrants would eventually disappear, either by returning to their homelands or by becoming absorbed in the societies of their adopted countries. In many cases they were considered a colorful, exotic addition not only to the street scene but also to the culture of these countries and their way of life.

The authorities in these countries had not considered the high birthrate of the immigrant communities or their inability and lack of desire to become integrated. The host governments were quite unaware of the social, cultural, and political consequences of welcoming people whose customs and values were so different from their own—immigrants who thought their values were superior and would want eventually, as their numbers grew stronger, to impose these values on the host countries. Nor did the Europeans foresee that these ambitions on the part of the immigrants would generate opposition, strengthen radical xenophobic parties, and add greatly to domestic tensions.

The Europeans' humanitarian intentions had been praiseworthy, but they did not anticipate that a high price would have to be paid for their innocence and naïveté. When they began to wake up to the realities, it was too late for radical solutions. They could with great difficulty deport a few agitators calling for violence, but the roots of the problem could no longer be tackled.

Islamophobia and Discrimination

THE TERM "ISLAMOPHOBIA" gained wide currency following the publication of a report in 1998 by the Runnymede Trust, a British organization devoted to combating racial discrimination and maintaining close relations between ethnic minorities. The working group dealing with dread and hatred of Islam and Muslims was headed by Professor Gordon Conway, a biologist, vice chancellor of the University of Sussex, and later head of the Rockefeller Foundation. The use of the term can be traced back to the 1920s, but at the time it did not catch on, whereas after 1998 it has been very widely used but also became a matter of controversy.

While the proponents of "Islamophobia"—that is, those who warned about the phobia—argued that there was a great deal of hatred of Islam and that attention should be paid to combating this phenomenon, its critics (in Britain, France, and other countries) maintained that the warning was little more than a public relations stunt, for there is no European collective psychosis, no special hatred vis-à-vis Islam as a religion, which is a subject of indifference to Europeans. In the Middle Ages, Christians regarded Muslims as an enemy mainly because of the Muslim conquest of the Holy Land. Muhammad was usually described as a false prophet, but Christian attitudes toward other religions, such as Judaism, and toward heretical sects within Christianity were far more hostile. In later centuries, Islam simply did not figure in European thought, except perhaps among professional theologians. More recently, Christian churches have gone out of their way to look (usually fruitlessly) for an ecumenical dialogue with Islam. Europe was threatened by Muslim invasions—in the West in the eighth century, in the East in the sixteenth and seventeenth centuries. But these invasions generated little, if any, *odium theologicum*.

If there was growing animosity toward Muslims in Europe in recent years, it was not in response to their religion per se but due to the fact that most terrorist attacks were carried out by Muslims; "terrorophobia" would have been a more accurate term, and if those involved in terrorism had been Eskimos, dread and fear would have been directed against them, even though the overwhelming majority of Eskimos had not been involved in the violence. If the condemnation of a few is transferred to a whole group this is of course unfair but probably inevitable, especially if a significant part of the whole group does not clearly distance itself from the "activists" among them or discourage violence but, on the contrary, expresses support or at least understanding for the terrorists. According to public opinion polls in 2005, a majority of Muslims in countries such as Jordan and Nigeria and 38 percent in Pakistan made it known that they had at least some confidence in Al Qaeda, and so did significant minorities in European Muslim communities. Violent anti-Western rhetoric and emphasis on the necessity of jihad (holy war) certainly did not help matters.

A few examples should suffice. There were few complaints among European Muslims in 1997; in fact, the very term "Islamophobia" was coined only the year after. Four years later there were three times as many complaints about religious or ethnic slurs. There is no secret why this sudden rise occurred: It was the escalation of terrorism. In contemporary Russia, not a country known for excessive love of outsiders (xenophilia), the government supports the Muslim Azerbaijani authorities, whereas the Christian Georgians are considered hostile in view of their struggle for independence from Moscow. A recent study on Spanish hostility toward Muslims, sharply condemning it, notes that it is "interesting to point out that the sub-Saharan immigrants, many of them Muslims and coming from very different cultures, are not included in this negative perception." True, almost 80 percent of Spaniards and Germans (and almost as many Swedes) thought Muslims fanatical and violent, but this trend developed as the result of terrorist attacks. The image of black African Muslims in Spain, for instance, was positive; the reaction was mainly directed against

Muslims from North African and Middle Eastern countries. In Britain as in other Western countries there has been no antagonism against Sufi and other Islamic sects who distanced themselves from violent action (see Gema Martín Muñoz in Jocelyne Cesari's *L'Islam dans les villes européennes.*)

There has been resentment and even hostility against newcomers in most societies, especially in countries that historically have not served as a shelter for new immigrants. The question arises whether negative feeling toward Muslims has been more pronounced than against other groups of immigrants and, if so, what might have been the reasons. True, there was in Britain in the 1970s a phenomenon called Paki bashing, in which young white working-class youths went out of their way to provoke and beat up Pakistanis in London's East End.

On the one hand, such attacks, however reprehensible, have appeared in many countries at various times, and the bashing ceased as the number of Pakistanis grew and as they offered resistance. On the other hand, attacks by Muslim immigrants against other groups in Europe have become considerably more frequent in recent years. (According to a poll in 2005, more than 40 percent of British Muslims expressed the opinion that Jews in Britain were a legitimate target for terrorist attacks.) In Germany in 1992, temporary homes of new immigrants (mostly Asians and Africans) were attacked and torched by youth gangs, sometimes of neofascist persuasion. On other occasions immigrants were beaten up and in a few instances even killed. However, these were xenophobic attacks directed against people from black Africa and the Far East or, in some cases, German repatriates from the Soviet Union who retaliated using violence. There was nothing specifically Islamophobic about these incidents. Similar attacks took place in Russia even more frequently, where they were directed often against migrants from the Caucasus, quite irrespective of whether the targets were Muslims from Azerbaijan or Christians from Georgia or Armenia.

Physical or verbal attacks in Europe against Muslim immigrants happened, according to reports by the European Union, almost always after major terrorist incidents such as 9/11 or the March 2004 bombing in Madrid or the London attacks in July 2005. Such attacks took various forms—graffiti was scrawled on mosques or Islamic institutions; women in *hijab* were verbally abused; Muslim children were called Osama. There were also "vitriolic attacks on asylum seekers" in the media and molestation of non-Muslim men and women. The "vitriolic attacks" complained of were usually nothing more than the identification by the news media of the often considerable part played by these immigrants in crimes that had been committed (as in the drug trade, etc.), with the stress on the identity of the perpetrators.

It would be interesting to know in this context whether there was more anti-Muslim graffiti than defacing of churches, synagogues, and Jewish cemeteries. But such statistics hardly exist, and if they existed, it would still not be clear whether the motive was ethnic or religious hatred. A Pew Research Center project of 2006 reached the conclusion that Muslims in predominantly Muslim countries are much more critical of Westerners than vice versa and that the same was true, albeit to a lesser extent, with regard to Muslim communities in Europe. In other words, there is considerably more phobia vis-à-vis Westerners and things Western than Islamophobia. If there were "vitriolic" attacks in the media on asylum seekers, it is not clear whether these attacks referred to innocent people trying to escape from a brutal dictatorship, or to "economic refugees," or to Islamists who had engaged in terrorist activities in their homeland. According to the number of arrests and court sentences, considerably more violence, ethnic and criminal, was generated by young Muslims than by "Islamophobes." Nor were banners and placards seen in public demonstrations calling for a holy war against Muslims.

It was argued, for instance, that the statement by an Italian prime minister that Western culture was superior to Islamic was an act of verbal aggression, and there was a dispute about whether, if these cultures were measured in terms of contribution to science and other such fields of human endeavor, the prime minister's assertion was a statement of fact. Such statements about the superiority of one culture (or religion) serve no useful purpose, but this was no Western monopoly; the theme of the superiority of Islamic spiritual values over Western decadence figured prominently in the sermons of Muslim preachers. If there was a growth in tensions and conflict, there was also far greater interest in Islam and its believers; more copies of the Koran were sold than in past decades.

One of the main complaints by Muslim organizations in Britain and elsewhere has been that young Muslims have been far more often singled out by police for identification under section 44 of the Anti-Terrorism Crime and Security Act (2001). More young Muslims than others were arrested as suspects and kept without trial. Such complaints have come from London but also from Paris and many other cities. Broadly speaking, antiterrorist legislation and practice is regarded as a direct attack on Islam or the Muslim community.

There are no official statistics that indicate whether the number of those stopped by police and sometimes arrested is indeed much greater than their part in the general population, but the impression that this is the case certainly exists. However, given the fact that terrorism has found supporters precisely on the fringes of the Muslim community and (since the end of terrorism in Northern Ireland) in no other group, the security forces could not have acted differently. To avoid the impression of racial or ethnic "profiling," police could (as in fact they occasionally did) stop as suspects elderly white ladies or severely handicapped persons or very old or very young people. But these attempts to appear evenhanded only invited ridicule. Given the fact that resources were limited, it was clear that such public relations exercises would not serve the cause of public order.

To recapitulate the list of Muslim immigrant complaints: They concern racism in prison, overcrowding, and discrimination on grounds of religion (even though this is banned by law). Fifty-four percent of Bangladeshi and Pakistani children live in homes that are on income support, that is, state support. Underachievement of Muslim children is another topic frequently mentioned in this context: Only 34 percent of boys achieve five grades at the General Certificate of Education, compared to a considerably higher proportion of girls (figures uncertain, but exceeding 50 percent).

To what extent could Western European authorities be blamed for discriminating against Muslim minorities? It hardly applies to social security assistance. While 5 percent of the population of Denmark are Muslim, they reportedly account for 40 percent of the social assistance outlay. The figures for other countries are similar (excepting only pensions and other categories that are not applicable). If they were to increase such payments and other help, this would be done on the backs of the non-Muslim, native underclass. It would lead (as in housing assistance) to further social and political tensions. Much of the blame has been put on social workers (for instance in Scandinavia), who have taught newcomers how to manipulate the social safety net. Some preachers have explained to their congregation that they have a right to get every possible payment and that only a fool would not make the most of the bounty available in Western societies. Instead of explaining to newcomers how to find work and the importance of education, they have created the impression among the immigrants that the state will take care of their needs, that it is obliged to help them since they are victims of an unjust world order, victims of colonialism, and so on. And thus funds were dispensed to the needy and to those who could have worked alike, and even the "militants" preparing for violent action were supported—not only the Kaplans in Germany but equally the suicide bombers in Britain and the Islamists of Scandinavia and Holland.

Pockets of poverty began to develop in the ghettos—more in France and Britain, less in Germany and Scandinavia. There was unemployment, especially among the younger generation, and the impression was created that hundreds of thousands of young men of North African, Turkish, and Arab origin eager to do almost any work were deprived of a chance for gainful employment simply on account of their names and where they came from. But no such complaints came from immigrants from India, including the Sikhs, or from the Far East; further, immigrants from Cyprus did not face the difficulties faced by those from Turkey. Construction workers, plumbers, and other artisans as well as nannies from Eastern Europe had the highest reputation in Western Europe and were at a premium. Caregivers from the Philippines were held in high esteem. Foreign construction workers were very much sought after, but those from Muslim countries were not a common sight on building sites. There was a considerable demand for people not only in the service sector of the economy, and those willing to work in these fields were not asked about their home address; it was immaterial whether their first name was John or Henry or Mustafa or Ali.

Much of the responsibility for this unhappy and unhealthy state of affairs could indeed be attributed to the authorities who had failed to direct the immigrants to productive work. These authorities had not focused on providing special education and professional training. True, it was not mainly the fault of the authorities if the young men dropped out of school and apprenticeships or if they failed to learn the language of the land (a problem throughout Europe but less so in England and France). And this leads to yet another question: Was there something in the social and cultural background of these families and individuals that prevented them from achieving as much as immigrants from other cultures? Much depended on the family background; if girls from these families did so much better in school than boys, was the reason perhaps that unlike boys, girls were not permitted to roam the streets in gangs for many hours? Or were the parents powerless to deal with their male offspring? Was it perhaps the fact that families from this religious and cultural background attributed less importance to nonreligious education than people from other countries? These and other questions have hardly been articulated, much less investigated; perhaps those who might ask such questions are afraid of being accused of racism.

Very often it has been argued that the Muslims' main complaint was the lack of respect toward them. Again, few such complaints were heard from other ethnic or religious communities. That every human being has the right to be treated fairly, not to be oppressed or offended, goes without saying. But those who were complaining about condescension or worse offenses wanted more—something that had to be earned by their achievements or their contribution to society. Their achievements were often poor and their contribution nonexistent, but still there was the demand for respect (or at least fear). There was no easy answer to this dilemma.

Politicians in America and Europe eager to pacify those who felt aggrieved went out of their way to emphasize in their speeches the importance and the eternal values of Islam. Those in Europe would not have dreamed of singling out Christianity, Judaism, Buddhism, or any other religion for such compliments; they also stressed the inestimable contribution made by the hardworking newcomers. Did they truly believe this or was it *taqi'a*—the practice of pretending? *Taqi'a* can be perfectly justified as a means of calming people at a time of great excitement and tension. But it seldom provides lasting cures.

In Britain some leading members of the Muslim community were knighted for their merits for the country; in countries lacking the British honor system, other awards were bestowed. But not everyone could be made a lord. All groups of immigrants throughout history have encountered some hostility until they were fully accepted; not one has started on the top of the social ladder in the new country. It is not easy to introduce a new system of advancement.

Euro Islam and Tariq Ramadan

SOME IN THE West have voiced high hopes for the emergence of a specific Euro Islam, a version of the religion that would take into account European traditions and conditions and would be compatible with them. Euro Islam has had no more prominent and eloquent representative than Tariq Ramadan. No one has appeared more frequently on television interviews and talk shows in Western Europe, and the cassettes containing his messages have been circulated in tens of thousands of copies. *Time* magazine included him among the one hundred most important intellectuals of the twentieth century; others have called him the Muslim equivalent of the

Reverend Martin Luther King Jr. Tariq Ramadan, the grandson of Hassan al-Banna, the founder of the Muslim Brotherhood in Egypt, was born in Switzerland in 1962 and is a Swiss citizen. In his youth he was an excellent soccer player and even played for Servette Geneva, one of the best Swiss teams. But he resisted the temptation to become a professional and instead turned to the study of Islam. He has appeared as a speaker in many countries and served as an adviser to Prime Minister Tony Blair in Britain but was refused entry to the United States and for a while also to France.

Tariq Ramadan's critics, comparing his writings and messages in Arabic and in European languages, have argued that "Brother Tariq" has made it a practice to preach a moderate, enlightened version of his faith in French and English and a more aggressive and radical message in Arabic. In brief, Tariq is as much a supporter of the Muslim Brotherhood as his grandfather, his late father, Said, and his brothers, all of whom were or still are very active on its behalf, and not just in the field of propaganda. Tariq has declared that he was never a member of the Brotherhood, but this is not a very meaningful statement, because the Brotherhood, unlike a political party, does not practice a Western-style bureaucratic "party membership" with monthly dues, membership certificates, and the like.

In his books (such as *To Be a European Muslim* [1999] and *Western Muslims and the Future of Islam* [2003]) and speeches Ramadan argues that with the growth of Muslim communities in the West, gradual change (perhaps even a silent revolution) is taking place that should make it possible for believing and practicing Muslims to keep faithful to their religion and yet live in harmony with their fellow citizens rather than to shut themselves away in a minority enclave. Given the character of Islam, the sharia (the religious law), and the instructions of the Koran on how to behave toward infidels, this is not an easy assignment and it is bound to involve Tariq Ramadan in many contradictions. He argues that he has no problem with a secular state and society, yet at the same time he bitterly opposed the French regulation banning the *hijab* in schools. He says that Muslims first and foremost belong to the *umma*—the community of believers—and they should do nothing that would make them bad Muslims. Yet he also says that the allegiance of Muslims in the West should be to the state and country in which they live. This would mean that they should obey the authorities as long as the authorities or society imposes nothing on them that contradicts their religion. In such cases there should be a "conscience clause" that allows them to state that certain actions or behavior is against their faith. This pick-and-chose approach as to what laws are to be observed can also be found among certain Christian sects (concerning, for instance, military service). But in the case of Euro Islam it would be much more far-reaching.

In contrast to radical Islamic parties such as Hizb al Tahrir, which maintains that Muslims should not become involved in the political life of their country of residence, at least not as long as they do not constitute the majority, Tariq Ramadan very much favors political engagement. His politics gravitate to the left—not of course to the Marxist, materialist left but to the New Left and third world radicals. His sponsors and supporters from early on have been figures such as the Swiss Jean Ziegler and Alain Gresh, an editor of *Le monde diplomatique* in France. Tariq Ramadan is a staunch enemy of globalization and stresses in his sermons the social message of Islam and the evils of capitalism, views shared by Hizb al Tahrir. These views are not systematic, however; they do not extend to something akin to religious socialism, nor has there been a demand that the ultrarich Muslims share with the poor.

Tariq Ramadan advocates not only an ethic of responsibility

but also partnership with other ecological and religious groups, various alternative organizations (such as the Association for the Taxation of Financial Transactions for the Aid of Citizens, better known by its acronym, ATTAC, for Association pour la taxation des transactions pour l'aide aux citoyens), and also groups defending human rights outside the Muslim community. Ramadan is aware that many Muslims, unsure of their identity, are reluctant to go too far in this direction. And it is indeed true that his ideas in defense of human rights have been the least successful part of Ramadan's teaching.

Ramadan's suggestions that Islamic injunctions in the field of business need to be adjusted to the needs of modern society have encountered little, if any, opposition on the part of the orthodox religious establishment. For if these antiquated laws were strictly applied, it would be impossible for Muslims to establish capital funds, make financial investments, or, on the personal level, use credit cards or take out insurance. But once Ramadan dealt, for instance, with the *hudud*—penalties imposed by the Koran and the sharia such as publicly stoning adulterers and apostates and amputating the limbs of thieves—he ran into serious opposition. Ramadan realized that the oppression of women is something like an Achilles' heel of Islam in modern Western societies and is in need of reform. But given the power of the religious establishment there was little he could do about it.

This was wholly unacceptable to the orthodox establishment, which included Qaradawi, the television sheikh of Al Jazeera and the friend of Ken Livingstone, the mayor of London. The orthodox establishment rejected Ramadan's views *tout court:* The *hudud* were part of the Koran and therefore not subject to change. In view of the family ties of Ramadan, however, his opponents agreed, with notable reluctance, to discuss some of his suggestions for reform. But the result could have been foreseen: His suggestions were unanimously rejected. As one of the legal scholars put it, if we call for a moratorium on stoning women and the death penalty, tomorrow there will be the demand to abolish the Friday prayer. (Ramadan had not asked for the abolition of the old laws, only a moratorium.)

One of Qaradawi's associates, a leading American Muslim theologian, declared that any tampering with the *hudud* was tantamount to the demolition of the Muslim nation and thus close to apostasy. Ramadan's argument that the norms of the Koran had been widely violated in the Muslim world by arbitrary authorities did not sway the religious establishment. The establishment was much stronger, and Ramadan had no wish to play the role of a radical reformer and possibly a martyr.

Many who had closely followed Ramadan's utterances did not believe in their sincerity and thought that in his heart he was still a Muslim Brotherhood member and the reforms he suggested were no more than cosmetic. One of his dissertations had consisted of a defense of the Muslim Brotherhood; he had attacked French Jewish intellectuals (including some who were not actually Jewish) for their critical attitude toward Islamism. And on essential issues he had never distanced himself from the Brotherhood and its fundamental tenets.

It could be argued in his defense that it was unfair to criticize him for duplicity, that this was unavoidable given his situation. He could not very well remain the idol of the Muslim Paris *banlieues* and at the same time of liberal intellectuals: He had to adjust himself to his audience, giving different talks, often inconsistent and even contradictory. While basically he remained a fundamentalist (as shown in his attacks against Muslim liberals and reformers), he understood that reforms were necessary to some extent if European Islam wanted to keep the loyalty of a younger generation exposed to Western influences. On occasion Tariq Ramadan openly admitted his dilemma. When in a television debate he was pressed on his stand concerning the stoning of women as a punishment for adultery, he would not dissociate himself from the practice but only replied that he would ask for a moratorium. His brother, a doctor of philosophy in Geneva and a teacher, justified stoning. Tariq Ramadan said afterward that had he condemned stoning, he would have made friends with French interior minister Nicolas Sarkozy but would have lost his following in the Muslim world and "once condemned, I can't change anything in the Muslim world."

This shows the limits of Ramadan as a reformer. His record has been contradictory; he has condemned terrorism in Europe, particularly in England. He wants European Muslims to be more self-critical but at the same time more conservative Islamic as far as their religion is concerned. He says he is against censorship but worked very hard (and successfully) for the banning of Voltaire's play *Fanaticism, or Mahomet the Prophet* (1741) in Geneva. There is not one Tariq Ramadan, but there are two and for the time being (and the foreseeable future) the Islamist Tariq is bound to be the stronger.

The story of a more liberal Islam does not begin and end with Tariq Ramadan. There have been many voices arguing in favor of a reinterpretation of the Koran, but they have come from North Africa and the Middle East, from India and Indonesia, rather than from Europe, which is not a center of Islamic religious thought. These reformers maintain that Islam is not antidemocratic but must be democratic, that human rights must be respected, that practices common in the seventh century are not binding for our time, that fatwas by orthodox Muslim leaders (often self-appointed) are not binding, and that individuals have the right to interpret the holy writs of their religion—and must have the freedom to think and express their opinions.

But these are at least for the time being minority views, even though the Internet has given the reformers a wider audience than they could ever have had in the past. The conservative, reactionary religious establishment is still strongly entrenched. Liberal Muslims are dismissed as inauthentic, even heretical, agents of the West. Paradoxically, reform Islam is weaker in Europe than in some Islamic countries, and the attempts of the French, British, and German governments to strengthen the liberal, progressive elements in the Muslim communities in their countries have not been very successful. This has to do mainly with the fact that among the Muslim immigrants to Europe there are relatively few educated people or intellectuals open to outside ideas; many of them, as with the Turks in Germany, emigrated from remote or traditional regions of their homeland—not from cosmopolitan centers. This could well change over time, but it is unlikely to change soon. Some reform of traditional Islam has became inevitable as the result of economic and technological development, but the conservatives are trying to limit the changes to this field. Even Osama bin Laden in his years in Sudan in the 1990s was a successful businessman whose practices were not really compatible with fundamentalist Islam.

Whether the fundamentalists will succeed in the long run in preventing the emancipation of women is doubtful. In their attempts to do so they are pointing less to religious arguments than to political arguments and to anti-Westernism—that they are a community under pressure from outside. But the roots of anti-Westernism are not purely religious. The danger facing Islamic traditionalists at the present time is not so much religious reform but religious indifference. With all the successes of fundamentalism in recent decades, they are aware (as one Berlin imam put it) that the way to the mosque is a long one and on this way young people face many temptations. The young may listen with enthusiasm to Tariq

Ramadan, but the majority of them no longer strictly observe many of the commandments of their religion, much less the five daily prayers. And this in the long run could be the real danger. The hold of the preacher on them is not as strong as on the generation of their parents.

Islamist Violence in Europe

TERRORISM IN EUROPE has a long history. It includes nationalist separatist groups such as the Irish Republican Army as well as left-wing and right-wing extremist groups ranging from Russian social revolutionaries of the nineteenth century, the anarchists of about 1890 to 1910, and the Baader-Meinhof gang of the 1960s and '70s to various neofascist sects. But since the 1980s this kind of terrorism has faded and been replaced by Muslim radical cells. Why did Europe become a target? According to the doctrine of Al Qaeda and allied groups, the United States and Israel, the big and the little Satan, are the main enemy. But Israel is difficult to attack for outsiders and so terrorism in that country has been left to the Palestinians. As for the United States, there was of course September 11, 2001, but ever since there have been no major attacks for a long time and there has been a debate whether the United States was Dar al Harb, the house of war, in which terrorist attacks were not only permissible but also desirable. For pragmatic or other reasons, most radical Islamists seem to have decided that attacks in the United States are not a major assignment at the present time. It also appears that with a few exceptions, such as the Schenectady, New York, Yemenites, it was not that easy to mobilize militants in the United States.

Nevertheless, Europe was not an obvious choice; one would

have expected more attacks against the "near enemy," meaning Arab governments such as those of Saudi Arabia, Egypt, and Algeria, considered hostile by the extremists. However, the terrorists were defeated in Egypt and Algeria, and, generally speaking, the terrorist leaders realized that attacks against foreigners would always be more popular in Arab communities than attacks against fellow Muslims. In the final analysis, Europe seems to have been chosen because it was easy to find recruits on the continent and because it was so easy to move and organize freely in the democratic countries. Reasons for such attacks could always be found; they could be explained as a punishment for helping the United States in its global war against terrorism and the invasion of Afghanistan and Iraq or because of the alleged persecution of local Muslim minorities.

Italy became of particular importance as a transit point to other European countries, as a departure point for fighters in Iraq, and as a logistic and financial support center. Many of these activities took place on the periphery of Milan's two Islamist mosques, Viale Jenner and Via Quaranta. Italian security forces asked the judiciary to deport several imams deeply involved in these extracurricular activities. But in some cases the judges refused to comply because they saw these "activists" as freedom fighters—or refused simply in order to annoy and frustrate the government of Italian prime minister Silvio Berlusconi. Italy carried out dozens of arrests of militants who had been helpers of the Egyptian al-Gama'a al-Islamiyya, the Algerian Salafist Group for Call and Combat, the Iraqi Ansar al Islam, and other groups. Italy was also a transit country for Muslims from Bosnia and in particular from Albania, but few, if any, of these were involved in political-terrorist activities.

According to French experts, there is a competition in recruitment of "activists" between various groups such as the Salafis (which were strong in the 1990s in Egypt and North Africa) and the *tabligh,* who have concentrated on religious education in a radical fundamentalist vein and also focused on conversions to Islam. (A few converts played a notable role in terrorist activities.) Some of these groups have trained their members for action inside France, others for operations in Iraq, the Caucasus, and other places abroad. By and large, terrorist action within Europe has been relatively limited. There are a number of possible reasons for this. Perhaps there were not sufficient recruits, and it could be that French counterterrorism efforts have been successful. It could also be that those terrorist activities that took place (in 1984–85 and the mid-1990s) seemed in retrospect ineffective and thus pointless. But past experience does not necessarily offer clues for the future, for each five or ten years a new generation of potential "militants" arises that is less influenced by past events than current concerns. The fact that terrorism in the past was not very successful, or not successful at all, may not necessarily be a deterrent, for their historical memory is short.

It is difficult to establish to what extent terrorists in Europe were directed from afar and coordinated. It was known that the March 2004 attack in Madrid was planned and carried out by a Moroccan group, that the Algerians were active above all in Italy and France, that Arabs were active in Germany, and so on, but to a considerable extent these activities followed local initiatives. There was, of course, mutual help between the various groups, but for this purpose no central leadership was needed. Local contacts could be found through mosques, clubs, bookshops, and such. Thus it was misleading to name Al Qaeda as the puppet master in each (or most cases), as the media frequently did. The old leadership of Al Qaeda was on the run and hardly in a position to plan and prepare complicated operations in countries far away from their hideouts in Afghanistan and Pakistan.

The Muslim networks developed in the 1990s. They consisted partly of "Afghanis"—men who had fought in Afghanistan and later returned—including some from Algeria and other Arab and North African countries, but also local militants. It has frequently been argued that the most likely candidates for terrorist missions were young unemployed men belonging to certain mosques or clubs affiliated with these mosques. They would be picked by a recruiting agent who promised them purposeful actions that would give meaning to their lives, not to mention excitement. The role of street gangs was important in this context. Others were recruited by fellow inmates of prisons.

However, the factors of poverty and unemployment are not sufficient explanations. Not a few terrorists recruited in Western Europe came from middle-class families and were studying for a first or second degree. This was the case with the network in Hamburg, which prepared the September 11 attacks on New York and Washington. The killer of the American journalist Daniel Pearl had studied at the London School of Economics; also educated were Mohamed Boujeri, the killer of Theo van Gogh, and many others such as Khaled Kalkal, the French terrorist militant of the 1990s, and Zacarias Moussaoui, the so-called twentieth 9/11 hijacker, who was caught in the United States. The more educated were frequently recruited through the Internet, which, as time went by, became an important recruiting ground for the jihadists.

If social and economic motives are insufficient as an explanation, political-psychological factors ought to be considered. Religion certainly played a role, but from what is known by no means the most pious and orthodox opted for violent action. According to a British report of 2005 prepared by the Home and Foreign Office, most of the middle-class recruits were loners attracted to university clubs based on ethnicity or religion who felt disillusionment with their current situation. Some were recent arrivals from North or East Africa, but there were also second- or even third-generation British citizens whose families had come from the Indian subcontinent. In addition, the report states, a significant number came from liberal nonreligious Muslim backgrounds or were converted in adulthood—including a few native British citizens and West Indians. All this tends to show that it must have been a mixture of motives—hatred of America, the West, and their own adopted country; free-floating aggression and the urge to gain "respect" (and, if not respect, at least fear); and complaints about double standards applied by their new home country in world politics. Why the inaction about Chechnya, Kashmir, Palestine, and other conflicts? But all in all, too few "activists" were involved and analyzed by the Home and Foreign Office to draw far-reaching generalizations about their background and motives.

It is not easy to understand, for instance, the motives of Turks, both in Turkey and in Germany, who welcomed with great enthusiasm both anti-American (and anti-Western and anti-Jewish) movies (e.g., *Valley of the Wolves*) and novels in which a combined Turkish-Russian nuclear attack against the United States was described. America, after all, had supported Turkey when it resisted Soviet territorial demands after World War II; it had supported Turkey's bid for entry into the European Union against considerable European resistance; and it helped save Muslim lives in the Balkans. Perhaps it was the propaganda of the spiritual leaders of these communities according to which America was the main enemy, even if neither Russians nor Arabs had ever been great friends of the Turkish nation (let alone pan-Turkism). It is even more difficult to understand why Nigerian Muslims would kill dozens of Nigerian Christians following the publication of the Danish cartoons in early 2006. None of the customary explanations concerning colonial repression, Western paternalism, or lack of respect applied in these and other cases.

Why had the European countries brought these attacks upon themselves? Above all, it was naïveté that had made possible the indiscriminate immigration of earlier decades. Europe was chosen as a giant safe house by terrorists because unlike all other parts of the world (including nations of North Africa and the Middle East and other Muslim countries), it offered not only security but also financial assistance because as political asylum seekers the "activists" were entitled to financial support according to the existing rules.

Thus a grotesque situation developed: Abu Qatadah, believed to be Osama bin Laden's representative in Europe, was given asylum in Britain. Abu Hamza al-Mizri made the Finsbury mosque the center of "militant activities" in Western Europe; Mullah Krekar, leader of Ansar al Islam, made his home in Norway. Abu Talal al-Qasimi, one of the heads of the Egyptian al-Gama'a, made Denmark the basis of his operation (1993); Abdel Ghani Mzoudi and Mounir el-Mouttazadek of the Hamburg cell that had carried out the 9/11 attacks continue to operate freely. They were arrested and detained for a while, but the German legal system was powerless to deal with them. Terrorist cells emerged and were active over many years in Madrid, Turin, Milan, Frankfurt, Rotterdam, Eindhoven (the Al Furqan mosque), and many other places.

In some instances "militants" were brought to trial, but more often than not they had to be acquitted. Most of them had lived on social assistance for years and received apartments, cash payments from local or state authorities amounting to tens of thousands (sometimes hundreds of thousands) of dollars, and unemployment benefits for them and their large families; in some cases they received support for their religious activities. Mullah Krekar, the leader of Ansar al Islam, was arrested by the Dutch authorities for a short period; he sued them and was paid 5,000 euros for wrongful arrest; this sum was later increased to 45,000. All the while, these activists made no secret of their intentions—indeed, they threatened the host governments with dire consequences unless their demands were met.

In most European countries (as well as in the United States, Russia, and India), antiterrorist legislation was somewhat strengthened after 9/11 and subsequent terrorist attacks in other countries. But even then the authorities were largely powerless to arrest or sentence suspected terrorists. If they did so, they were denounced as acting illegally by not only local human rights watch organizations, Amnesty International, and so on, but also European political institutions—usually with reference to the European Convention on Human Rights.

Terrorism was often defined as asymmetric warfare, and as far as the law was concerned it certainly was. If Islamists engaged in propaganda calling for murderous action, this could frequently be considered permissible under the freedom of speech laws. If they prepared for a terrorist action, they could perhaps be arrested and held for a few days, but they could hardly be sentenced because no harm had been done. It could always be argued that they had not really meant to carry out the terrorist act. Thus it was argued that even in the United States, those who carried out the attacks on September 11, 2001, could perhaps have been detained for a short time but not prosecuted, let alone found guilty, until they had actually taken over the airplanes for their final mission. If they were found in possession of weapons, this was of course illegal, but the sentences were bound to be lenient. Even weapons of mass destruction (especially if these were binary weapons, i.e., materials that could also serve peaceful purposes) were not necessarily conclusive proof. If membership in a terrorist organization was proved beyond any reasonable doubt, it could be argued that this was a guerrilla band protected by the Geneva Convention or a movement of national liberation (as happened in Italy), membership in which was not a punishable offense but worthy of support.

More often than not the evidence against suspected terrorists either was inadmissible in court because it had been gained through various intercepts or would have involved the security forces' revealing the sources in open court, which in most cases they refused to do. Of all the European countries, only France had a system that was capable of dealing more or less effectively with terrorism, and it also followed up prosecution with sentences and deportation. As a result, many of the terrorists who had originally found asylum in France, legally or illegally, transferred their activities to "Londonistan" in the 1990s. In almost all other European countries, deportation proved to be extremely difficult legally and therefore exceedingly rare. Those found to be a danger to the state could not be deported to their countries of origin because most countries outside Europe (including the United States and most Asian and African countries) had not abolished capital punishment and there was always the danger that they would be treated roughly, even tortured. It took years to extradite terrorists even from one European country to another in which they were wanted, and in some instances such extraditions, for whatever reasons, never took place. When in contravention to these laws a few were extradited or deported after all ("rendition"), all hell would break loose. How could one treat inhumanely people who had to be considered innocent until found guilty? The situation was further complicated because some of the suspected terrorists were not foreign nationals but naturalized citizens.

Naïveté, the incapacity to understand the terrorist danger, has been mentioned as the main reason for the liberal attitude toward asylum seekers out to engage in violent action. It was thought to be un-British (or un-Scandinavian) to refuse refuge to people who claimed to be in acute danger in their countries of origin. There was perhaps also an element of bad conscience dating back to the 1930s, when all these countries had refused asylum to the genuine refugees from Nazi Germany. But there were almost certainly also other motives at play. In Britain for instance, Islamic radicals were given to understand that if they refrained from "illegal" action, that is, appeals for terrorist action inside the country, their presence would be tolerated and their other activities would be overlooked. This unwritten covenant seems to have been in force for years, and similar understandings appear to have existed in other European countries. A case could also be made in favor of the proposition that as long as the activities of violent Islamists were not banned, they might be easier to observe than if they had been compelled to go underground.

These calculations based on the "beggar thy neighbor" principle seem to have worked in some cases but not in others; they did not, for instance, prevent the London attacks in July 2005. Generally speaking, the attitude of European countries toward terrorists and their fellow travelers was one of toleration as long as they "behaved"; following major terrorist attacks, tougher measures were introduced. But as major attacks were not very frequent, demand for the abolition of such measures would always grow as memory of the attacks faded. There were many individuals and groups who believed that the terrorist danger was greatly overrated (perhaps even exaggerated by the authorities) and that the preservation of human rights was the most important duty, even if it put human lives at risk.

In their struggle against terrorism, European governments received little help from the Muslim communities. The head of Scotland Yard's antiterrorism division announced in September 2006 that British security forces were tracking thousands who were suspected of planning, financing, or encouraging attacks. The spokesmen of the British Muslim communities traditionally claimed that either the security forces were mistaken or, more likely, they intended to blacken the reputations of innocent people.

IT COULD WELL BE TRUE that the most critical issue facing Europe was not only, or not primarily, terrorism. Even if there had not been a single bombing in Europe, there are still the profound demographic, social, and cultural changes that are taking place. Furthermore, there are Islamist organizations that officially dissociate themselves from the Al Qaeda–style activities but still believe in jihad and other forms of violence. In some respects they resemble the fascist movements of the 1930s, which had also believed in mass violence, dominating the street, rather than in acts of individual terrorism.

This refers for instance to Hizb al Tahrir ("party of liberation"), which was founded in Jordanian Jerusalem in the early 1950s. Like most of these organizations, Hizb al Tahrir was an offshoot of the Muslim Brotherhood, which they considered not sufficiently anti-Western. It is rabidly anti-Semitic ("and kill them wherever you find them," in the words of the Koran). However, Hizb al Tahrir has been claiming that its statements have been quoted out of context. It has reportedly tried to operate both as a legal party and as a secret underground organization, and this has resulted in doctrinal and other complications. Hizb al Tahrir is certainly a fundamentalist and radical organization (though according to its version Islam is a rational religion); its principal aim is the restoration of the Caliphate (or Khalifat), which was abolished with the abdication of the last Turkish sultan in the 1920s.

The Hizb and its even more radical offspring only recognize

the *umma,* the worldwide community of Muslim believers, and think that nation-states and borders between them are artificial. These extremists claim that they do not support terrorism even though individual members have taken part in terrorist operations and even suicide missions, and they have welcomed Al Qaeda operations in their publications. They have been well organized and quite strong in certain Muslim communities, threatening their rivals and opponents in the community with unspecified consequences. They envisage a situation in which they seize power, presumably by violent means, at a time when they will be strong enough to do so by having infiltrated the state apparatus.

Unlike other radical Islamist groups, the Hizb al Tahrir is an elitist organization that recruits educated cadres. It began its existence in Britain, where it is fairly strongly represented on university campuses like Birmingham, Bradford, and the London Imperial College. It would be wrong to think of the Hizb al Tahrir as a group of intellectuals and ideologists, however. Rather, its membership consists of technicians and their like. It is not strongly represented in France but is quite active on the territory of the former Soviet Union, especially in Central Asia. While even more radical groups have engaged in deliberate provocations ("we shall hoist our flags over 10 Downing Street"), Hizb al Tahrir seems to believe such actions counterproductive.

Hizb al Tahrir is one of several Islamist organizations operating in Europe; there has been and continues to be a great deal of splits among groups of this kind. Hizb al Tahrir has been charged by some of its enemies in the same camp as being agents of Western imperialism—and has accused them of the same. This possibility can by no means be excluded. It can be taken for granted that most of these radical groups have been infiltrated by the security services and rival Islamist groups; whether their activities are manipulated by outside factors is, of course, unknown. Be that as it may, their very existence shows that European societies are facing the threat of violence not only on the terrorist level operated by small underground cells but also by political organizations that will try, once the time is ripe, to launch mass violence. Hizb al Tahrir has been banned in most Middle Eastern countries (except Lebanon, Jordan, and the Gulf states) and in many European countries, but as far as Europe is concerned, this seems not to have greatly curtailed their operations.

This brief survey of various Islamist groups left out of our purview one important category of violence, namely, spontaneous violence, as seen in the riots in Paris in November 2005. While most of those who took part in these riots (or the earlier communal riots in the British Midlands) were Muslims, there is no evidence that they were instigated by any specific organizations according to a master plan. The riots were the result of "objective" conditions on one hand, the mood of the young generation in the ghettos, and, on the other hand, of course, the indoctrination by preachers and political agitators. But this is not to say that the political agitators were in a position of either starting the unrest or putting an end to it. And it is quite likely that a similar situation will recur in the future. Nicolas Sarkozy, the French minister of the interior, mentioned the presence of two to three thousand *casseurs* (breakers), mainly based in the Paris *banlieues,* who often engage in vandalism and violent action: torching and smashing property, stealing, and mugging. While the majority of *casseurs* come from the Muslim suburbs, they also include a few militants of the extreme right as well as some anarchists. In the words of Sebastian Roche, a French political scientist, they are basically apolitical, outside the political process, believers in violence for violence's sake.

THREE

The Long Road to European Unity

SINCE WORLD WAR II, POLITICAL Europe has changed almost out of recognition. After uncertain beginnings, the movement toward greater collaboration and unity made considerable progress in the 1950s and '60s, advanced fitfully, ran out of steam, then regained some momentum. But the movement came to a halt in 2005, when France and the Netherlands, two of the European Union's founding members, turned down the proposed constitution that had been submitted for a vote. The prospects of a united Europe remain uncertain. To discuss these prospects, the road so far has to be recapitulated, however briefly. "The construction of the European Community ranks among the most extraordinary achievements in modern world politics, yet there is little agreement about its causes," said Andrew Moravcsik, a leading student of the Community.

The idea of Europe as an entity separate from Asia and Africa goes back to ancient times, but it was not a problem that greatly preoccupied Greeks or Romans. During the Middle Ages and thereafter, various books and pamphlets were published concerning Europe, but it was an issue of greater interest to geographers than political philosophers. This began to change in the seventeenth century when French finance minister Maximilien de Béthune, the Duc de Sully, William Penn, and a few others gave thought to the need to establish a European organization or perhaps even a parliament to preserve the peace on the continent, which during that period had been sadly violated by the Wars of Religion (1562–98) and the Thirty Years' War (1618–48). The idea was taken up a hundred years later by Charles-Irénée Castel, the Abbé de Saint-Pierre (1658–1743), in his book about perpetual peace, *Le projet de paix perpétuelle* (1713; A Project for Setting an Everlasting Peace). The Abbé de Saint-Pierre's ideas found their way to Rousseau, Kant, and other thinkers of the Enlightenment. The basic idea was the need to preserve peace, which, it was believed, could not be guaranteed simply by trusting the peaceful intentions of rulers and the equilibrium between the various powers.

With the French Revolution dawned the age of national states, and while the idea of European unity did not entirely disappear from view—it can be found in Mazzini's concept of Young Europe and Victor Hugo's United States of Europe—the stress was on nationalism rather than internationalism, on war and expansion rather than on international cooperation. Individuals such as Richard de Coudenhove-Calergi (1894–1972) continued to advocate such ideas for mutual security as Pan-Europa, but these proposals were theoretical constructs; the masses could be mobilized by nationalist movements, not by abstract schemes. Hitler and Mussolini were stronger than Aristide Briand and Gustav Stresemann (the foreign ministers of France and Germany, respectively, the leading protagonists of peace in Europe, who shared the Nobel Peace Prize in 1926). The European right was doctrinally averse to cosmopolitanism, but among the left, too, there was no enthusiasm: Lenin had denounced the idea of a United States of Europe during World War I. True, even Hitler invoked the idea of a unified Europe, but this was toward the end of his life when the war went badly and help was needed against the Soviet Union and the Western allies. In any case, his idea was for a Europe under German leadership.

For some Europeans it was not at all obvious why they should get closer together. They spoke different languages and had different traditions and ways of life; what separated them seemed far more important than what they had in common. Germany and France had been enemies since time immemorial, and so were Germans and Slavs. There was no love lost between Britain and the Continent. There were no United States of Asia and Africa—not even of Latin America (which, with one exception, did speak a common language)—so why should there be a United States of Europe? The nation-states, after all, had grown organically. Europeans were willing to work, to sacrifice, even to die for their country, but there was no such feeling of loyalty vis-à-vis Europe as a whole.

It took World War II and its disasters to give fresh impetus to various initiatives aiming at closer unity. The governments-in-exile

of Belgium and the Netherlands decided to form a closer union
(Benelux, i.e., Belgium, the Netherlands, and Luxembourg), and
there were other such schemes; cooperation was in the air. But it
was above all economic necessity that acted as the main engine in
the movement toward unification. Jean Monnet, a central figure in
this movement who helped lay the foundation for the European
Economic Community (the Common Market) and later the European Union, once said that crises are the real federators, and postwar Europe certainly faced a major crisis. (On another occasion,
many years later, Monnet said that if he were to start again with the
business of unifying Europe he would probably start with culture
rather than the economy.) But such was the devastation at the end
of the war that it seemed unlikely that the countries of Europe
would recover through their own efforts.

Help from outside was needed, and this could come only
from the United States, but there were other preconditions for a recovery, and they included close cooperation between the countries
of Europe, the lowering of customs and tariffs, the liberalization of
trade, and other such measures. America favored the plans for European unity and so did Britain, even if Churchill suggested that
the United Kingdom should stay out of it. The Soviet Union,
which had been invited to participate, opposed it, regarding it as a
dangerous challenge to Soviet plans for the future of Europe. But
such was the need for closer cooperation that Russia, too, eventually established an organization for closer economic collaboration
named Comecon, which linked the Union of Soviet Socialist Republics with East Germany, Czechoslovakia, Bulgaria, Poland, and
other nations in its sphere of influence.

These then were the circumstances in which the European
Union was born in 1950–51, initially an association preoccupied
with the production of coal and steel, with France, Germany, Italy,

and Benelux as founding members. True, it was not only the economy that acted as a federator. These were the years of the early cold war, Communism's takeover in Eastern Europe, the Berlin blockade and airlift (1948–49), and the outbreak of the war in Korea (1950). There was the need to defend Western Europe, which the individual countries left to their own devices were not able to do. Hence the various initiatives to establish a European defense organization. But these projects were unsuccessful and the defense of Europe was left to the North Atlantic Treaty Organization (NATO), founded in April 1949 as an alliance between the United States, Canada, and ten European countries—later joined by Turkey and Greece (1952), Germany (1955), and others.

When the first steps were made toward European unity after World War II, the idea of a common foreign and defense policy did not figure; this appeared only much later in the late 1970s but soon lost impetus. The movement toward a common market, however, gained momentum. For many years French president Charles de Gaulle blocked the entry of Britain. But in 1972 the United Kingdom and Denmark joined, followed by Spain, Portugal, Greece, and so on; the six became nine, later twelve and fifteen, and after the fall of the Soviet Union another thirteen joined. The Council of Europe came into being as well as a European parliament, a European court, and a central bank, the European commission, and the European Atomic Energy Community (Euratom) and many other common institutions. In 1962 a common agricultural policy was decided upon—one of the most controversial decisions ever taken and one that would later cause endless disputes. Eventually a common currency, the euro, was introduced (2002). There were milestone meetings, such as the one at Maastricht in the Netherlands in 1992, where the Treaty on European Union formed the European Union, and others of lesser importance. It was no secret that those who joined the European Union did so for economic reasons; it was a going concern and no one—or hardly anyone—wanted to be left out.

Naturally, every nation was out for its own interests, and the paramount question was "What's in it for us?" There were unrealistic expectations and some unjustified complaints. To give but two examples: The smaller European countries complained that their interests were disregarded and the greater powers were running the European institutions as if they belonged to these powers alone. Seen in retrospect, however, the smaller European countries—such as Ireland, Austria, Spain, and Portugal—benefited quite well economically from the Common Market. They received substantial help at critical periods; whether they would have done equally well outside the "Eurosphere" is at least doubtful. Another source of complaints was the introduction of the euro. When it was first introduced it was worth U.S. $1.18. Within less than a year it fell to 90 cents. As these lines are written it is $1.25. But most Europeans were less interested in the comparative value of the euro and the dollar; there was the perception, not unjustified, that the introduction of the new currency made life more expensive.

There were waves of Europessimism (also called Euroskepticism, Eurosclerosis, and Europaralysis) beginning in the 1980s, partly because the Common Market did not work so well as had been expected. True, customs were abolished, but there were many other ways to hamper liberalization, for instance by introducing nontariff obstacles that would make foreign competitors adhere to specific national standards and conditions. If Brussels interfered, however, there were again complaints about undue and unnecessary meddling. True, visas had been abolished and there was free movement within Europe, but such a situation had prevailed (except in Russian and Turkey) even before World War I. Some complaints had less to do with the working of the Common Market than with the general economic situation. In the early years of the Common Market there had been steady, even spectacular growth all around; in later decades there was slow or no growth. Unemployment had been unknown initially, but toward the end of the century it became a serious problem.

An interesting and disquieting process took place toward the last years of the twentieth century and continued thereafter: an increase in the number of Europeans critical of the United States and especially of U.S. foreign policy. The disapproval rate reached 58 percent in Germany, 62 percent in Spain, 66 percent in France, and 41 percent in the United Kingdom; the score was about the same in Sweden and the Netherlands. Greece and Turkey agreed on little else, but their opposition to U.S. foreign policy was high—between 70 and 80 percent.

There were many points of contention. The Americans—that is, the administration of George W. Bush—refused to sign the Kyoto Protocol to the UN Framework Convention on Climate Change (global warming), proposed in 1997 and effective in 2005, even though the United States is the leading emitter of greenhouse gases. Further, the United States declined to sign the treaty establishing the International Court of Justice developed by the United Nations. There were constant disputes between the United States and Europe about the legitimacy of European agricultural subsidies and steel tariffs, but also disagreements about world political issues such as the Arab–Israeli conflict. At the time of the second Iraq war (2003–), opposition to U.S. foreign policy in countries such as France and Germany increased even more, as well as in many of the smaller countries; the disapproval rate was around 80 to 90 percent.

Given such opposition, one would have expected that many or

most Europeans would have expressed strong support for a united Europe. But when asked in 2004 how they would react if Europe ceased to exist tomorrow, less than a third of the inhabitants of Britain (but also of Eastern Europe) said that they would regret it. Only 54 percent of Europeans said that membership in the European Union was a good thing; one year later this had declined to 48 percent—and to 28 percent in the United Kingdom. This mood extended also to the new members; as the president of the Czech Republic declared in 2006, what Europe needed was more democracy, not necessarily more unification. Even in countries where protest against their own government was not a major factor, enthusiasm for Europe waned. Only 33 percent of Austrians were still in favor of membership in the European Union in 2006; a year before it had been 42 percent. The figures for Finland were similar.

John Gillingham, a historian of European integration writing in 2003 (two years before the acute crisis of 2005 surrounding the "no" vote by France and the Netherlands), summarized the state of affairs and the prospect of united Europe as follows:

> The future of Europe and of European integration is today in jeopardy. The EU has accomplished little or nothing in the past ten years, the public is alienated from it, and policy makers have shown themselves unable to head off disaster over enlargement. Privatization and marketization have come close to a standstill. The regulatory authority of the EU, indeed its very legitimacy, is contested.*

But such pessimistic voices were few at the time, among both the academic experts and the Eurocrats in Brussels. There had

---

* John Gillingham, *European Integration 1950–2003* (Cambridge, 2003).

been warning signs well before. In 1992 the Danes, albeit by a very small majority, had rejected ratification of the Maastricht Treaty, which caused both great astonishment and indignation in the major European capitals. (The Irish, too, voted "no" in another context in 2000, which came as a surprise to many.) French president François Mitterrand foolishly decided on a French plebiscite on the same lines, which was wholly unnecessary because a simple vote in the French parliament would have been sufficient. Mitterrand prevailed in the end—with 51 percent, not a famous victory. Not only in Euroskeptical Britain but all over Europe there was a backlash against the elites who wanted to impose their policies on a population who had not been consulted.

Whether the Brussels projects were sensible and in the common interest was quite irrelevant: The popular discontent stemmed from a great variety of sources, last but not least from opposition to their own governments, which were blamed for the worsening economic situation. Another important motive was the reluctance to hand over national sovereignty to central, remote, and anonymous institutions over which people had no control. Some European countries had obviously benefited more from the Brussels projects than others. To what extent had opposition to the movement toward closer unity to do with this? In some cases it was quite obvious. If many Spaniards voted in 2005 in favor of a European constitution, this could be explained with reference to the fact that Spain had greatly benefited from the support it had received, which made its economic development possible.

But economics certainly did not explain French opposition, for France (not only French farmers) had also been among the main beneficiaries. Furthermore, France had played a disproportionately influential role in all European institutions. On the international scene France had played a leading role precisely because it was thought to speak on behalf of all of Europe. The Netherlands, all things considered, had not suffered from European unification, the country had been among the founders of the European Union, and it had been considered all along a model country as far as the European common spirit was concerned. And yet the Dutch voted against the proposed EU constitution.

Some of the growing Europessimism that led to the crisis of 2005 had to do with the diminishing popularity of the various governments from the left as well as those from the right. There was much talk at Brussels about a "European model" that set the continent apart from the United States and from other continents. This referred mainly to the welfare state, and it is true that there was a consensus on these lines. Even a conservative like former British prime minister Margaret Thatcher would not dare touch these social services. But it was no more than a broad consensus and, furthermore, it was precisely at this time that reforms and cuts had to be made in the welfare state. More and more frequently questions were asked as to which of the services of the welfare state could still be afforded at a time of slow or no growth and a rapidly aging population. There was no conviction that more union was urgently needed. There seemed to be no outside enemies as there had been during the cold war. Nor were other threats looming greatly in the public consciousness in the years just before and after the turn of the century. The fact that formidable economic competitors had arisen in Asia had not yet registered. Islamism seemed a distant danger. Terrorism was considered largely a problem for the United States.

All things considered, the Common Market seemed to work tolerably well. Thus it was not at all clear why it should be necessary to surrender more sovereign rights as envisioned by the Eurocrats. But the political elites were not aware of the popular mood. They had decided in Maastricht on a Common Foreign and Security Policy (CFSP) as one of three pillars of joint security (the other two pillars concerned economic and social policy and justice and home affairs), but as often happened, this agreement was little more than a statement of intentions. As the Saint-Malo declaration of December 1998 put it: "The European Union needs to be in a position to play its full role on the international stage. . . . To this end the Union must have the capacity for autonomous action backed up by credible military forces." This proposition, British and French in origin, was endorsed at a Cologne meeting six months later. But in fact little, if anything, happened. France seemed to be interested in such a common policy only to the extent that it could largely dictate the policy, as had been the case in the past. But with the broadening of the European Union this was bound to become more and more difficult. Europe had shown disgraceful impotence during the Balkan crises (first in Bosnia, later in Kosovo) of the 1990s. These conflicts occurred, after all, not in some distant part of the globe but in Europe's backyard. And yet, but for the military power of the United States nothing at all would have happened. Europe, the "quiet superpower," sent military observers—who were arrested by the local armies—and these observers looked on helplessly as tens of thousands of civilians were massacred.

Following the failure in the Balkans, another summit in Amsterdam in 1997 decided to streamline the decision-making process in foreign policy as well as to establish a policy planning and early warning unit. But this was another dead-end summit because the European Union had no military capacity. Following further meetings in Helsinki (1999) and in Nice (2000), it was decided to establish within the next three years a European military unit consisting of 60,000 soldiers as well as 30,000 air force and marine personnel equipped with 100 vessels and 400 aircraft. All forces

should be ready for action within sixty days. But they were sched-
uled mainly for keeping the peace in crisis areas as well as perform-
ing various humanitarian tasks. There have been various crises
since then, such as the ongoing genocide in the Darfur region of
western Sudan, but this force has not intervened. But even if this
intervention force had been sent to Darfur, of what use was a unit
that would take two months to become ready? It had become a farcical situation.

How to explain the failure to establish a common foreign and
defense policy? Partly it has to do with the cumbersome structure
decided upon. Various policy guidelines were decided upon as well
as mechanisms for regular political dialogue, and special representatives were appointed for crisis regions. But far too many bodies
were involved in the elaboration and implementation of the Common Foreign and Security Policy (CFSP)—the European Council,
the Council of Ministers, the president of the Council, and so on.
In addition, a number of new structures were set up such as a High
Representative for CFSP, a committee of permanent representatives, and a Political and Security Committee (PSC), as well as at
least seven more committees and subcommittees. So many authorities could not possibly act rapidly and effectively even if they had
military resources at their disposal.

But even if there were a chain of command that would make
quick decisions and even if there were a European army, there still
would be no unanimity between the various countries on policies
and strategies. Up to the end of the cold war (and after), NATO
provided a shield for Europe. But NATO had been dominated by
the United States, and with the breakdown of the Soviet empire it
seemed to many that NATO had lost its raison d'être, even if few
put it in such blunt terms. European interests were by no means
identical with those of the United States. But even in the 1990s and

thereafter, some European countries were in favor of cooperation with the United States (the Atlanticists—Britain, the Netherlands, and Eastern Europe), whereas others, such as the French and the German Social Democrats, wanted a counterforce to the United States. Still others, such as Austria, Sweden, and Finland, were neutral (or neutralist) in their orientation.

Some European countries cooperated with the United States in the Gulf War and the Iraq war, while others opposed the wars. But even those who wanted to set up a force separate from NATO and the United States were not really willing to make the political, financial, and military effort needed to set up a combined unit of this kind. In theory this should not have been too difficult. The European countries had armies totaling some 1.5 to 2 million soldiers, 22,000 tanks, and 6,500 aircraft. Had they decided to delegate just one-quarter of these forces, a substantial military force would have come into being. But technical difficulties aside, there simply was not the political will to do so, nor was there any feeling of urgency. On the contrary, virtually all European countries were reducing military spending during the 1990s and the following decade and thus reducing their military capabilities. Britain and France are nuclear powers, but could it be assumed that they would put their nuclear arsenal at the disposal of a European army? In brief, after all these deliberations and decisions Europe did not exist as a military power.

Between Washington and many European leaders there were fundamental differences in approach as to how to deal with current problems in world affairs, and the exchanges became more and more acrimonious. This was the famous "Americans are from Mars, Europeans from Venus" debate. According to Robert Kagan's frequently quoted essay "Power and Weakness" (in *Policy Review,* June 2002), European attitudes such as the belief in the

United Nations and diplomacy as the most effective instruments for solving world crises were described as reflecting not so much "national character"—no one would have argued in 1940 that Europeans are from Venus—as Europe's reduced status in the world. Europe saw the contemporary world as one in which laws, rules, and international cooperation were increasingly decisive, whereas military and even political power was gradually discarded. The rule of law was becoming the norm not only in domestic policies but also in international affairs. Brute force, according to some American Euro-optimists, belonged to the past as the world moved beyond power politics. European statesmen and political theorists were criticizing America for mocking and deriding the United Nations, the supreme authority and the best hope for a peaceful world (what with Pakistan, Cuba, China, Russia, and Saudi Arabia on the new UN Human Rights Council). The peaceful European example with its democracy and social model was bound to have a domino effect as far as the rest of the world was concerned, in the view of the American Euro-enthusiasts referred to earlier. Europe would eventually be successful in promoting a new world order of peace, justice, and freedom, whereas America's aggressive policy was bound to fail. Military power had been discredited in the twentieth century. Europe had learned the lesson and had become a moral superpower.

Whenever a real crisis arose, however, be it in the Balkans or the Middle East, it soon appeared that neither Tehran nor even Slobodan Milošević was impressed by Europe's status as a great civilian power and that without American military help Europe was not capable of achieving anything. It took weeks of bickering to summon a peacekeeping force for Lebanon in the late summer of 2006—a force far smaller than the 15,000 troops UN Secretary General Kofi Annan had requested.

Whether U.S. strategy concerning the export of democracy

would succeed or fail is a different question; what is of relevance in the present context is the European philosophy. Was it genuinely believed that the future belonged to European soft power, or was that merely a rationalization of weakness? This is not easy to answer. Given the realities of the world in the early twenty-first century, with aggressive religious and nationalist trends not only in distant countries but also on Europe's very doorstep; given Europe's demographic and economic weakness, unemployment, and the dependence on oil; given the failure of European initiatives in the Balkans and the Middle East, as well as the disquieting developments in the former Soviet Union, it seems difficult to believe that anyone could have seriously thought that the twenty-first century would be Europe's. But one should never underrate the power of wishful thinking. It was a truly Eurocentric concept based on growing European cooperation in the postwar period and the fact that a war among the European countries had indeed become unthinkable.

Perhaps it was also based in part on the assumption that America's aggressive foreign policy was bound to fail, that it would result in a retreat of the United States from world politics, some form of neoisolationism. But all this could not possibly explain the belief in a world in which soft power would prevail. It was a worldview oblivious of the spread of nuclear weapons, of the growing likelihood that weapons of mass destruction would be used, of the impotence of the United Nations on one hand and the emergence of uncooperative regimes such as the Iranian and North Korean on the other. In brief, it was a belief based on the assumption that the rest of the world was like Western and Northern Europe, and if it had not quite yet reached this stage, it would reach it very soon, for Europe and the rule of law were the envy of the rest of the world.

It was a worldview so far detached from realities that its mainsprings and motives remain a riddle. The development of the EU has been a matter of great interest to political scientists, constitutional lawyers, and others. Theory builders had a heyday, above all those dealing with integration, the neofunctionalist school had its say, but so, too, did the intergovernmentalists; supranational governance, including the issue of multilevel governance, became a hotly debated issue. But while these theorists were absorbed in these fascinating discussions there was the danger that the concerns and the mood of real people would be ignored—as indeed they were.

This then, very briefly, was the situation when the vote against the European constitution plunged the European Union into a deep crisis. The problem of enlargement (the question of whether or not to include Turkey) generated yet another crisis. One could, of course, explain the negative vote as a "populist backlash," and this explanation was by no means entirely wrong. The opponents to closer European cooperation included the far left and the extreme right (in France some 75 percent came from the left) and various antiglobalist and antidemocratic elements. Opposition was often based on national egotism or on the most backward and reactionary elements, who had forgotten nothing and learned nothing from recent European history.

But this was only part of the story. Brussels had taken popular support for granted. And if the "Euroenthusiasts" in their dreamworld truly believed that Europe was already a (moral) superpower, being the envy of the rest of the world, then why should they undertake efforts to strengthen its defenses?

FOUR

The Trouble with the Welfare State

GREAT CRISES FREQUENTLY COME AS a surprise unless they happen in the wake or as the result of a major war. There were perhaps no immediate reasons in the 1990s to suspect anything untoward concerning the future of Europe. True, there were basic unresolved issues that should have made for caution. But influential circles were voicing great optimism—not only the Brussels Eurocrats but also the national governments from Berlin to Paris and beyond.

And then there were the American academics and think tank

experts who had persuaded themselves that the twenty-first century would be Europe's. What if there was some unemployment and the economic indicators had not been too brilliant for some time? Perhaps after decades of rapid progress the continent needed a pause for consolidating its achievements, after which it could continue its strong advance. And even if progress in the future would be slower, this was no reason for despair: An economic miracle with its great growth year after year seemed unnecessary and perhaps even undesirable. There seemed to be no particular hurry to force the pace; after all, in most games there is an interval to give the players time to recover and regain fresh impetus. What was true for a game of soccer or ice hockey was even truer for such a serious undertaking as building a new Europe.

Europe had been declared dead or dying countless times during the last two hundred years, but it had always surprised the doomsayers by its vigor. France had been considered a spent force after its military defeat by the Germans in 1870–71, and there had been many tracts about the sad fate of the *grande nation* ending with a lapidary statement: *"Finis Galliae."* And yet within thirty years France had recovered and pervasive pessimism had given way to a new optimism. Oswald Spengler's *Decline of the West* had been the bestseller of 1919 (and for years thereafter), but Spengler had been dealing with the cyclical fate of high civilizations over long periods in history. Jean-Paul Sartre and his friends had written about Europe dying in convulsions after World War II, but postwar developments in Europe defied these predictions. Instead of collapsing it had made a fresh beginning, resulting not just in much greater well-being of Europeans but also in a fairer, more civilized society than at any time in the past. And if there were some warning signs in the 1990s, there were also indications for great hope. With the breakdown of the Soviet empire, Europe, which had been divided since World War II, could at long last draw together again. But such growing together was bound to take time; it could not and should not be rushed.

Only gradually did the understanding begin to sink in that what had seemed to be at first a temporary "time-out" went on and on and that neither national governments nor Brussels (the European Union's headquarters) seemed to have answers to the problems facing Europe. It was also during this period that the desire was gaining ground in Europe to follow an independent policy, distinct from America, in a world that had changed. But as the years passed by it also became clearer that the idea of a civilian superpower had been a chimera, that political and military power still counted in an unquiet world and that the countries of Europe were not willing to undertake the efforts needed to become a power to be reckoned with in the world. They had not become reconciled to the idea that to become an effective force in world affairs they had to surrender sovereign rights and at the same time increase their defense capacities. "Soft power" was fine as an alternative to military power, but Europe did not have much of either.

When should the alarm have been sounded? Up to the time of the first oil crisis (1973), the performance of the European economy had been excellent, with growth rates of 5 to 8 percent in Germany, 4 to 5 percent in France, and 5 percent in Italy as the norm; only the United Kingdom (2.5 percent) had been lagging behind. In the midseventies there was a substantial downturn: Inflation rose to 10 percent or more, and unemployment increased and remained relatively high.

The 1980s were the years of "stagflation" (stagnation accompanied by inflation), but the general picture was uneven; some countries did better than others. During the nineties there was a slow recovery, but another slump took place in 1992–94. Among the best performers were the United Kingdom, Spain, and Ireland—

countries that had been lagging behind in earlier decades. Various reasons were suggested for the very much slower economic growth, such as "Eurosclerosis" (sluggish and rigid labor markets), but it was also clear that the stormy growth of the postwar period was bound to slow down in any case: New jobs could not be created indefinitely, and exports could not be boosted forever, because there were limits to growth. In fact, unemployment was rising steadily: It exceeded 10 percent in all major European economies but Britain, and in Spain it exceeded 20 percent. Whatever policies were applied, it proved exceedingly difficult to reduce unemployment.

In the years after 1995, growth in Europe was slow (little more than 2 percent) but relatively steady; unemployment, however, continued to grow. There was a great deal of talk about the urgent necessity for reform, particularly in Germany and France, two of the countries most affected. But little was done; there was too much political resistance.

It is fascinating how differently the state of affairs was viewed by economists of different persuasion. As Philippe Legrain observed in 2003 in *The New Republic*, living standards have risen over the past three years by almost 6 percent in the European Union but only by 1 percent in the United States. Productivity growth in several European countries was higher than in the United States, Germany had higher productivity levels than the United States, and even unemployment was lower in some European countries than in America.* If Europe suffered from a cyclical downturn, this did not imply long-term decline. Europe's strict labor laws were not really a great obstacle to growth; despite their existence, some European countries had outperformed the United States, and in any case, they were about to be reformed. In brief, the truth about Eu-

*Philippe Legrain, "Europe's Mighty Economy," *The New Republic*, June 16, 2003.

rope was that its weaknesses were not as big as they seemed and the advantages were underplayed. The euro was soaring and the long-term boost to growth from the creation of a genuine single market with a single currency would be huge.

This was one way to look at the situation, and the Lisbon resolutions of the European leaders in March 2000 (mentioned in the introduction) were in a similar vein. But many took a far darker view of both Europe's current situation and its future prospects. A CIA report in 2005 predicted the collapse of the European Union within ten to fifteen years unless radical reforms were undertaken. In France books appeared with titles such as "The Collapse of France" (*La France qui tombe*) and, in Germany, "Can Germany Still Be Saved?"

Were these economists and political commentators writing about the same continent? The pessimism about Europe was summarized by Robert Samuelson in an article titled "The End of Europe" (*Washington Post,* June 15, 2005) and by Fareed Zakaria in "The Decline and Fall of Europe" (*Newsweek,* February 14, 2006). Samuelson drew attention to the discrepancy in birthrates between Europe and America and pointed out that by 2050 one-third of the population of Europe will be sixty-five or older. Apart from high unemployment and slow growth, how could the European economies operate in the future with so many elderly people heavily dependent on government benefits (necessitating high taxation)?

European benevolence was admirable, but it required a strong economy. (A similar problem existed in the United States, but the birthrate there was considerably higher.) Above all, many Europeans lived in a state of delusion: They thought that somehow, even with all the problems, life would continue as before. Almost any change or reform seemed a menace. The EU constitution had been rejected even though it did not imply any radical changes—but it had become the lightning rod of all kind of European discontentment.

Fareed Zakaria, commenting on a detailed report by the Organisation for Economic Co-operation and Development (OECD) in Paris published in early 2006, mentioned the assessment of the OECD's chief economist that if current trends continued, the average U.S. citizen would be twice as rich as the average Frenchman or German. The argument that Europeans valued leisure more than Americans and that as a result, even though poorer, they had a better quality of life did not persuade Zakaria. If they would be only half as well off as the Americans, this would mean poorer health care and education and diminished access to all kind of other goods and service and a lower quality of life. Necessary reform in Europe had been postponed time and again, paralyzed by strikes and protests, and the efforts to liberalize trade had also been violently opposed. European higher education and scientific research, once foremost in the world, had been steadily declining. In some fields, such as the biomedical sciences, it was no longer on the map and might well be surpassed by Asian countries. All this meant a further reduction of Europe's position in the world. At the same time, less defense spending weakened its ability to be a military partner of the United States or even to project military power for peacekeeping purposes. The weakening of Europe meant that it could not be a serious rival to America and America's superpower status would linger on. But it was also bad for the United States, as Samuelson put it, because it weakened the world economy. Europe could no longer be a strong ally of the United States because of the commitments required of an ally: "Unwilling to address their genuine problems, Europeans are becoming more reflexively critical of America." This gave the impression that they were active on the world stage, even as they were quietly acquiescing in their own decline.

It is interesting in retrospect to read the impressions of some American observers such as T. R. Reid, head of *The Washington Post*'s London bureau and author of *The United States of Europe: The*

New Superpower and the End of American Supremacy (2004). Reid described how he had to take his young daughter to the emergency room of a London hospital soon after his arrival. After only fifteen minutes' wait, a gentle nurse and an authoritative doctor saw Reid's daughter and competently dealt with the problems. When he took out his checkbook the nurse smiled at his mistake and told him crisply and proudly that things were done differently in Britain and that he would not have to pay for medical treatment.

Reid and his daughter were lucky; the normal waiting time in an emergency room in the United Kingdom is a few hours, and the likelihood of seeing a competent doctor is uncertain. But he could have mentioned other impressive achievements of the British welfare state, such as the fact that education, including higher education, even the study of medicine, was free and that senior citizens in London could travel for free on urban transport. But he should have perhaps also mentioned that taxation in Washington was lower than in Britain (even though London was a far more expensive city than Washington), that social security payments were higher in the United States, or that American medical doctors once qualified would earn twice as much or more than in Britain.

Reid said in the preface of his book that Americans, including official Washington and almost the whole political class, had been asleep as a new kind of superior political entity had emerged in Europe. Americans simply did not face up to the rapidly growing power and authority of the EU government in Brussels. They were in a state of denial. Not long after Reid's *United States of Europe,* another book appeared that warned of the dangers of sleeping while important historical processes were taking place: *While Europe Slept* (2006) by Bruce Bawer, with the subtitle (which said it all) "How Radical Islam Is Destroying the West from Within." And a third book, *The Hour of the Asians (Die Stunde der Asiaten),* by Jochen Buchsteiner, complained that a somnolent Europe (in contrast to

America) had somehow never realized that a major change had taken place in world affairs, with China, India, and other Asian countries as leading economic and political powers. As a result, Europe had been marginalized; it was now a mere onlooker.

The Europhiles in America and their colleagues in Europe were not all wrong in pointing to Europe's many social and cultural achievements and the attractive qualities in its way of life. They also were not wrong in stressing that the United States was in some respects scandalously lagging behind or that there were differentials, sometimes obscene, in income. There were other notable differences. Martin Hüfner in *The Power of Tomorrow (Europa, Die Macht von Morgen,* 2006) rightly stressed the beauties of the European landscape. Some of the "twelve European values and characteristics" that he listed to prove Europe's predestination to be the power of tomorrow were less obvious. Was it really true that Europeans (in contrast to Americans) were more inclined to think ahead and plan for the future? Were Europeans really more tolerant toward other opinions and religions? Were they more internationalist?

Dominique de Villepin, the French prime minister who coined the phrase "economic patriotism" when he opposed the merger of some big French corporations with other European enterprises, would probably not have agreed. As far as the record of the absorption of new immigrants was concerned, there was not that much that America could learn from Europe. It was certainly true that Europe had less of a feeling of mission. But there was another side to the coin: Polls were showing that most European countries were not particularly proud of their own traditions, values, and way of life. In fact, if the polling results were correct, Europeans' self-esteem was somewhat low.

The Euro-optimists were fundamentally wrong not only in overrating European economic strength but also in focusing relentlessly on a comparison between Europe and the United States. For even if their critique of America would have been justified, it did not necessarily follow that the European achievements were secure and would last. Above all, the impression was created that the United States was the main rival and competitor of Europe whereas in reality the competition came from the newly industrialized nations.

The welfare state figured very prominently in all these discussions. Its origins, the idea that in a civilized society there must be a safety net for the weak, go back far into history. Its sources in Germany are in the legislation mainly with regard to social and medical insurance established under Chancellor Otto von Bismarck. In England in its modern form it was the plan developed by Sir William Beveridge during World War II, which provided for a unified national system of social insurance and comprehensive national health care, with the aim of eliminating want and poverty. As contemporary economists see it, the modern welfare state redistributes income from the working young to the retired old and from the rich to the poor (Assaf Razin and Efraim Sadka). According to a classic definition by Asa Briggs (now Lord Briggs), the British welfare state guarantees a minimum standard, including a minimum income, and provides social protection in the event of job loss and services at the best level possible. This is the theory. In practice, services are at a low level and have to be rationed according to the funding available. The character of the welfare state varies from country to country. In France, much of the budget covers pensions, which, as in Germany, are (or were until recently) relatively high. In Sweden and other Scandinavian countries the welfare state is most ambitious, offering a social minimum to all citizens.

Social expenditure is high and has risen over time in all European (and all developed) countries. In 2001 it was 27 to 29 percent of the gross domestic product in Denmark, Sweden, France, Germany, and Belgium and over 20 percent in all other major European countries, including the Southern Europeans (Italy, Spain, Greece, Portugal) and some Eastern Europeans (Poland, Hungary, and the Czech Republic). Countries outside Europe had a considerably lower ratio of welfare expenditure: 18 percent in Australia, New Zealand, and Canada; 17 percent in Japan; 15 percent in the United States; and 14 percent in Ireland. However, these lower figures are somewhat misleading because in the United States and Canada, for instance, a higher percentage than elsewhere of health insurance was covered by the private sector.

The achievements of the European welfare state have been remarkable; Americans can only dream about a thirty-five-hour working week or five weeks of paid holidays a year—in Denmark they were striking for six weeks. Some critics were saying that the safety net had become a safety hammock. There was growing criticism (not just from those on the ideological right) about growing abuses of the welfare state by parasites—that in fact in certain respects provisions of the welfare state were inducing parasitism in society.

But these abuses were not the real issue; they could be corrected with a certain measure of oversight. The real problem was that all these social assistance programs were affordable without great effort as long as substantial economic growth took place. For many years now the future of the welfare state in Europe has been under pressure until it has become the most important domestic issue: *le trou dans la Sécu*—the hole in the social security services. Not, of course, because there was enormous ideological opposition, for no politician, however conservative, could afford to run on an anti-welfare-state platform. The reason was that the welfare state over time became more and more expensive and the reasons were, of course, well-known. People were living longer and more pensions had to be allocated. Medical services became more and more expensive. With rising unemployment, more support had to be given to those out of work. The number of students has grown fivefold, tenfold, or more all over Europe since the end of the Second World War, and more funding had to be given to schools and universities. In brief, everything became more expensive and there was an obvious limit to the level of taxation that could be imposed by governments. The tax rate reached 45 percent in France and Italy and even higher in some other European countries.

Various strategies for how to cope with this problem have been discussed over the last two decades, such as gradually raising the age of retirement. But given the size of the problem—the share of the elderly in the population will double by 2050 and the share of the employed will decline sharply—there will have to be a reduction in old-age pensions. Medical services are rationed and allocations for education have also been cut. This has been bitterly opposed by the political left and the unions, but they have not been able to provide alternative strategies to raise the funds they think are necessary and at the same time keep the economy afloat (including sustaining the rate of saving and investment).

How can the slowing down of the European economy during the last two decades be explained? Various theories have been put forward. One of the most recent and influential has been Mancur Olson's theory about the rise and decline of nations (*The Rise and Decline of Nations: Economic Growth, Stagflation, and Social Rigidities,* 1982). According to Olson, small coalitions pursuing specific interests find it easier to push through policies that favor them than do big groups acting in a wider interest. These policies of small groups are likely to be protectionist and will hamper technological innovation and thus have a negative impact on economic growth. One could think, for instance, of Western European peasants and steel producers in this context.

But it is doubtful whether such a theory can provide more than a partial explanation. The European crisis would certainly have been less acute or in any case less strongly felt but for the emergence of the new economic powers in Asia—first Japan, later the East Asian "tiger states" (such as South Korea, Taiwan, and Malaysia), then China, and eventually India. Japan and the tiger states were showing signs of weakness in the 1990s from which they have since recovered.

The economic performances of China and India were most impressive. With growth rates of 10 percent and more, China has risen to be the third largest trade power in the world, and India has reached a growth rate of 7.3 percent. Europe benefited from the rise of these new powers in various ways—exports, investments, and joint ventures. But it was also clear that these exports would not continue indefinitely on the same level, and Europe frequently found it impossible to compete with the ever-increasing and ever more sophisticated imports from countries in which the production costs were so much cheaper than the costs in Europe.

How could the European social model survive in an economic world order in which Europe had to compete with countries that could produce goods so much more cheaply? Did it mean that "Asian conditions" would eventually prevail in Europe? Such issues as these, and not the question of when Europe would overtake the United States, became the central and most worrisome concerns in Brussels and the European capitals. As the Asian economies would grow, the standard of living would also significantly increase, but it would take a long time before it would reach the European level. The current per capita income is $770 in India and $1,700 in China, compared to $30,000 to $40,000 in the major European countries.

But is it certain that economic trends and indexes offer the master key to the rise and decline of nations? History does not offer a clear answer. They are of importance, surely, for weak and backward economies cannot sustain a country or keep a continent politically active. But economic factors alone cannot explain the rise and decline of big powers and small; these factors cannot even always account for major economic trends. Whether the mood of a nation is optimistic or pessimistic, whether it has great hopes for the future or tends toward despair, seems to depend on a great many factors. Gibbon in his *History of the Decline and Fall of the Roman Empire* (1776–88) saw perhaps the single most important factor in societies immersed in slothful luxury losing their vigor—why make great efforts if life has become so easy? To a certain extent, decline could be a question of generational change.

How can we explain the decline in the birthrate at a time when having children has become economically more affordable than ever before (and when many young women would like to have two or three children)? Could it be because young people are afraid of the future, as many have argued, or because (as equally many have suggested) they want to enjoy life without the burdens of child rearing and because the institution of the family has eroded and the divorce rate has reached 40 percent? It is estimated in Germany that to bring up a child to his or her twentieth year costs approximately half a million euros. But most of these funds come from the state or the local communities, and if our great-grandparents had thought of such financial considerations, most of us would not be alive. Many questions and no conclusive answers.

Germany

GERMANY IS STILL the strongest economy in Europe and was for many years the main engine driving the European Community. But even before the crisis of the last decade a distinct skepticism, even pessimism, had prevailed in the country. Since the Second World

War there has been an inclination in Germany to react more nervously than other European countries to any political or economic setback, even minor ones, and this was accompanied by an equally strong tendency to ignore long-term threats. In the 1980s it was connected with the fear of a new world war: A mad American president (Reagan at the time) was pushing the world to the brink of war, and there were mass demonstrations in the streets, which could create the impression that the day of judgment was near. But the world was only near the end of the cold war. However, many of the German political class did not learn from their misjudgments and their pessimism found other targets—the United States again, or the market, or globalization.

All this was no doubt connected with Germany's history in the twentieth century: defeat in two world wars, the trauma of the inflation, the Great Depression of the 1930s, and the experience of Nazism. But other European nations also had their traumas and yet did not overreact.

True, the German economy did face serious difficulties, which are well-known. For a decade or more per capita income had declined, and unemployment persisted on a high level: When Chancellor Gerhard Schroeder came to power in 1998 he promised to reduce unemployment to 3.5 million; when he resigned six years later, the figure was almost 5 million. In the words of one of his chief academic advisers, Germany had become a slow-motion society. The growth rate had declined since 1995 to an annual 1 to 2 percent (less than in most other European countries), and during a few years there had been negative growth. Germany was still an exporting giant, but the future looked uncertain. Domestic consumption remained low. The cost of reunification was to be much higher than originally assumed. The transfer (of capital) from West Germany to the East amounted to 4 percent of the gross domestic product throughout the nineties and thereafter. Nevertheless, the residents of East Germany *(Ostdeutsche)* felt discriminated against, while those in the West felt exploited by their inefficient compatriots in the East (whom they sometimes referred to disparagingly as "Ossis"). The high and rising price of oil was yet another factor impeding economic growth.

Even the predictions of the experts were subject to wild fluctuations. In mid-2005 *The Economist,* the weekly bible of the political-economic class, published an editorial announcing that everything had changed, or was about to change, predicting a positive, if not brilliant, future for Germany. Six months later, in an even longer article, *The Economist* said only a miracle could save the country.

Where to look for the causes of the malaise? Was it the fact that Germans, once known as hard and solid workers, were no longer working very hard and that as a result of short hours and high wages the costs of production had become so high as to be no longer competitive? Indeed, some leading German corporations had for this reason shifted some of their factories abroad to places where production costs were much lower. That Germans now work fewer hours than the residents of almost any other nation is an undisputed fact. But other European countries (admittedly smaller ones) with equally high living standards had managed to create new jobs. Or could the malaise be attributed to the fact that many of the young, the more enterprising, and the more highly educated and innovative had found that their chances to succeed were substantially better abroad, above all in America, and that Germany had lost these people?

Under Chancellor Schroeder an overall scheme called Agenda 2010 was prepared to restore the German economy's competitiveness by lowering the costs of production through lowering wages. A committee was appointed, with workforce reformer Peter

Hartz as its head, to cut some of the social services, such as reducing pensions and unemployment assistance and limiting medical services that had been free earlier on (Hartz I, II, III, IV).

These were painful measures and they led to the impoverishment of some sectors of the population. The unions and the Social Democratic left bitterly opposed the cuts, and some even disputed the legality of some of these measures, which, they claimed, were in violation of the Basic Law of the republic (the constitution), which promised all citizens a life in dignity. But how could the state assure a life in dignity if it did not have the funds to do so? On the one hand, the left-wing opposition claimed that the government could help the economy by strengthening domestic demand, which was true enough, but it would have made exports even less competitive and it would have compelled the government to engage in even higher deficit spending. For the neoliberal opposition, on the other hand, Schroeder's reform measures fell far short of what was needed. Like other European governments, it was exceeding in any case the limits of budget deficits set by EU headquarters in Brussels (3 percent), and this meant a serious setback for the future of the European economy. Eventually, in late 2005, the Schroeder government fell because it could not find sufficient support for its policy. It was succeeded by a grand coalition headed by Angela Merkel, the leader of the conservative Christian Democratic Union, who became not only the first woman to serve as chancellor but also the first East German.

There is near unanimity in Germany that the old model no longer works and modernization and reform are the commandment of the hour. But there is enormous resistance because the majority quite rightly realizes "modernization and reform" would mean substantial cuts in the welfare state and a decline in the standard of living for most of them. They accept that this is unavoidable, but they do not want to be the ones to suffer. In the circumstances no political party and no coalition of parties is willing to engage in a course of action that would almost certainly lead to its defeat in the next elections. Support for a policy of drastic cuts can be expected only in response to a major, immediate crisis, not in a situation of slow decline.

But why have other countries, such as the Netherlands in the 1980s and Sweden in the 1990s, been able to carry through painful reforms that led to a certain improvement in the economic situation, a major reduction in the number of unemployed, and a decline in debt? It is probably easier to carry out such reforms in smaller countries than in large, more anonymous societies. The (relative) success of the Netherlands and Sweden may have to do with historical traditions also. In any case, a convincing answer to the question remains to be given.

France

THE ECONOMY OF France is the fifth largest in the world, and its problems closely resemble those of Germany. After years of spectacular success, governments of the right and of the left have failed for years to encourage growth and employment. As Nicolas Baverez points out, France is the only one of the developed countries that has not yet overcome the crisis of the 1970s (though he could have added Germany to his list). The country is more and more facing the danger of becoming a museum and a center of distribution, disconnected from production and research. This has reflected itself in a mood not so much of cosmic despair as of no longer believing in anything, least of all in promises by governments (this in the words of a secret report by local prefects to the central government, is the reason that the situation is relatively calm). According to public opinion polls, only 9 percent of the French believe that their country is making any progress. The rest are convinced that at best it is marking time or that it is declining. When François Mitterrand was elected president in 1981 he promised (as Schroeder would in 1998) that he would drastically bring down unemployment. When he left office, unemployment was more than twice as high as when he entered. Some economists believe that this problem will eventually be solved as the result of the falling birthrate, but even if this prediction is true, it is unlikely to happen soon.

The history of France has never been one of steady development but of periods of quick progress alternating with long periods of stagnation or decline. But it is doubtful whether accepting this fact offers much reason for optimism for the future, for stagnation has now lasted too long and its causes are too deeply ingrained to allow for basic change. A model that worked well in the 1960s (*dirigisme,* a kind of typically French semiplanned economy on the basis of a market economy) no longer works forty years later. It gave the French economy a much-needed push in the early days, but more recently it has not shown enough adaptability and innovation. True, there has been a certain retreat from *dirigisme,* but the French state still owns a larger share of the country's economy than any other in Western Europe: It is spending some 53 percent of the nation's GDP. There has been little privatization in France, which suspects the market and dislikes competition.

A welfare state has emerged that in its old form is no longer affordable, but opposition against change is even more emphatic in France than in Germany, manifesting itself in mass strikes and other such actions.

One of the peculiarities of the French economy is that a higher number of those employed belong to the public sector (25 to 30 percent); they are considerably better off than others, with regard to both wages and pensions; and they are willing to fight tooth and nail to hold on to these achievements. Millions of Frenchmen went to the street in 1995–96, not to express revolutionary class solidarity or defy a heartless anti-working-class government, nor to protest income inequality or combat the malign effects of globalization, but, in the words of a knowledgeable outside observer (Timothy B. Smith), to maintain their corporatist privileges. Such mass strikes have continued, on and off, to the present day.

While the social achievements of French workers were impressive, it was also true that they were limited to certain sections, more especially to those in key positions able to paralyze the economy. There has been (and is) widespread aversion and distrust toward the private sector, whose employees, except for some in the higher echelons, are less well paid and taken care of. The French model with its special interests and lobbies comes closest in many respects to the Mancur Olson model, even though Olson said that he understood the French economy least of all. To finance this kind of corporate welfare system (which excluded wide sections of the population), French governments had to go deeper and deeper into debt, but their attempts to stem the tide were bitterly resisted. The problem seemed intractable. When the thirty-five-hour working week was introduced in accordance with the Aubry laws of 2000, it was believed that this would have a beneficial effect in creating new jobs (the idea was to divide the labor among more workers), but this did not come to pass. When Prime Minister Alain Juppé wanted to raise the age of retirement in certain branches from fifty to fifty-five years, this saved some money but did not create new jobs, either. As Timothy Smith observed, the corporatist welfare state blocked job creation. Globalization was a popular scapegoat, but a closer look shows that only a small percentage of French workers were hurt by it.

Tourism is one of the flourishing branches of the economy,

and some economists see the future of the country in tourism and marketing. The impressions of tourists—unless they also visit some of the many ghettos—could be (superficially) of a beautiful and flourishing country. But this is misleading, for annual growth rates in the range of 0.9 to 2.0 percent are not enough to maintain France's place in the world; industrial production growth rates have been even lower in recent years. The political left and right in France agree that the productive sector of the economy has to be strengthened, new jobs created, and costs in the social security sector cut. Restrictions on competition in sheltered service industries and elsewhere reduce productivity. The left claim that many of the new jobs created are badly paid and too short-term; like many Germans, they do not want "American conditions" or Thatcherism in their country. But they do not offer realistic alternatives. Many years ago I listened to Raymond Aron declaring at a conference that France was witnessing revolutions from time to time but seldom, if ever, reform. At the time I thought it a bon mot, but there might have been more truth in it than I thought.

United Kingdom

AFTER THE END of the Second World War, Britain's economy performed poorly in productivity in comparison with other European countries. Germany and France overtook the United Kingdom and Italy had almost matched Britain's productivity by 1990.

By the 1970s Britain had become the new "sick man of Europe," but the harsh changes introduced by Prime Minister Margaret Thatcher (1979–90) caused radical change. She stood for a free market economy, privatization as far as possible, lower taxation, and reducing the power of the trade unions. This reached a climax with defeating the National Union of Mine Workers, which had foolishly declared a general strike at a time when mining was on a sharp decline.

Thatcherism led to a revival of the British economy—and to great hostility on the part of the left. Among the negative features of the Thatcher period were her relentless nationalism and opposition to continental Europe as well as the decline in the manufacturing industry that took place under her leadership. However, it is doubtful whether this might not have taken place under any government. Even Thatcher's bitter enemies could not deny that her policies had worked (Peter Mandelson said, "We are all Thatcherites now"). The British, individually and collectively, were certainly not worse off in the post-Thatcher period than before.

What followed under the Labour government, from the mid-1990s to about 2005, was the golden decade in British economic development. The growth rate in 2002 was 2.0 and in the years that followed 2.5, 3.2, and 1.9 respectively. By 2005 the British economy was the world's fourth largest and the United Kingdom was the world's twelfth richest country. There was steady growth, inflation was low, and its currency was strong. The rate of unemployment was among the lowest in Europe. The Organisation for Economic Co-operation and Development (OECD) praised the stability and resilience of the British economy and noted its flexibility. The fact that Britain was almost self-sufficient in energy because of the North Sea oil as well as coal reserves was one of the strengths of its economy.

Among the weaknesses of the British economy were a low rate of saving and a personal indebtedness of more than a trillion pounds sterling. Another weakness is the dependence on the building boom and the relative weakness of the manufacturing industry, which accounts for only 16 percent of the national output and, as in other European countries, has been slowly declining. By 2005 the economy was slowing down and its vulnerabilities were becoming more apparent. According to Anatole Kaletsky, author of *The World in 2006* (published by *The Economist*), there was no reason for gloom, provided the British government pursued a correct economic policy, which, in his view, meant cutting public spending rather than raising taxes. The forces that had made the golden decade possible were still operative: the competition in labor and product market, improving terms of trade, flexibility of monetary policy, growing demand for knowledge-intensive services, and so on. But it was an open question whether such a policy was politically feasible.

Political and psychological reasons quite apart, the relatively strong performance of the British economy (and of the pound sterling on the currency markets) strengthened in recent years those in the United Kingdom who doubted the wisdom of intensifying its links with the European Community.

Italy and Spain

A COMPARISON BETWEEN the development of the Spanish and the Italian economies in recent years is a study in contrasts. Under Francisco Franco (d. 1975) and for some years after, Spain was among Europe's most backward countries. But following its entry to the European Union in 1986 (and with considerable assistance), it made rapid progress and almost caught up with the average EU living standard by 2005. Its GDP now amounts to slightly more than a trillion dollars; the devaluation of the peseta made the Spanish economy competitive. Unemployment was reduced from 23 percent to about 10 percent. A highly centralized system was largely decentralized. Spain became not only one of the most successful European countries but also one of the most faithful in the European context—as the results of the elections concerning the European constitution have shown. Together with France it supported a neo-Gaullist policy for Europe, dissociating itself on various occasions from the United States.

The problems facing the Spanish economy were largely the same that confronted the other European nations: A rapid decline in the birthrate led to an aging of the population and consequently the need to reform the welfare state—above all, to reduce the pensions for the aged.

Italy had its economic miracle somewhat later than the other major European economies—in the 1960s and early '70s—but since then the country has fallen back, and for years its growth rate has been the lowest. Italian industry found it difficult to make the transition in time to high technology, the car industry has not been able to compete, and the textile industry was almost destroyed by Asian competition. Its main income is now derived from luxury goods (e.g., designer clothing, food, and cars) as well as tourism. The black market sector of the economy, traditionally strong in the south, has not had a decisive impact on the overall performance, except perhaps in reducing unemployment to a certain degree. As with Germany some of Italy's industrial production has been moved abroad in view of high labor costs. As in the other major European economies, there is general agreement that "things cannot continue as before," but there is enormous resistance to substantial reforms. The policy of a right-of-center government has been to blame the nation's economy on outside factors over which it has no control. (Left-wing governments have used exactly the same argument—blaming globalization.) A rapid decline in the birthrate and immigration, often illegal, from central and North Africa, have added to social tensions.

* * *

HOW MUCH LONGER WILL COUNTRIES like Italy, France, and the other major European economies be able to muddle through? Perhaps longer than widely expected; life for the majority of the population is still tolerable, often enjoyable, if ambitions are not too high. In the circumstances a slow, gradual decline seems more likely than a major collapse. As in the political life of these countries, the will to carry out far-reaching changes is missing; most likely it will be generated (if at all) following a further drastic deterioration, a clear and present danger. Such a situation may arise, but it is not certain. The deterioration could be slow, almost imperceptible, as long as (for instance) unemployment does not substantially exceed 10 percent. Or it could be too late for reforms, for by the time the necessity is generally accepted, the economies might have deteriorated too much to be salvageable (too late, in any case, to be carried in a democratic framework).

It is true that many of the economies of smaller European countries, such as the Netherlands and the Scandinavian nations, have been doing somewhat better than the big economies, but this does not decisively alter the general picture. Moreover, from time to time there are encouraging signs indicating brighter prospects for the future. If Europe's economic performance was sluggish in 2005, there were certain signs for an improvement in 2006/2007. German exports were stronger, and so were those from some other countries. But whether the growth rate is 1.3 percent or 2.0 percent, the basic problems persist. The financial debts of the major economies continue to grow relentlessly, domestic demand is still far too low, there is no chance that fuel prices will decline to any significant extent, and not enough jobs are being generated.

The economic prospects are largely unpredictable because the countries of Europe are very much dependent on one another—and on the United States and the Far East. Any downturn in these giant economies could have immediate repercussions in Europe.

One hesitates even to speculate about the political consequences of Europe's economic weakness. There are no enormous differences between the left and the right's proposals about the changes that should take place. Germany has a coalition government, and in the United Kingdom Conservatives and Labour, whatever their other disagreements, have no basic quarrels with regard to the economy. The French and Spanish left are more averse than the center to the liberalization of the economy and are more fearful of the market, but the force of conditions is such that they cannot follow radically different policies. If the moderate left and right should fail, there is of course the danger that mass support will go to extremist parties that normally would not stand a chance. But they, too, have no magic formulas; the hour of fascism and communism is over—in Western, Central, and Southern Europe, at any rate.

It is a sad situation in which there are few prospects for a decisive turn for the better. The only question is whether there will be slow deterioration or a rapid collapse. It used to be said about Europe that it was an economic giant but a political dwarf—and now there is the danger of its gradually losing its economic-giant status. In these conditions one might do worse than retiring with the books published only yesteryear on the brilliant postwar period when there was so much optimism in the air or, better yet, with one of the recent publications that told us Europe would be tomorrow's great power. There are always possibilities one might have overlooked that could be indicative of a much better future. It could be that more international investments will go to Europe than in the last decade or two, but to what branches of the economy would investments go—to tourism or high technology? Seventy-five million tourists visit France each year, 52 million visit Spain, and 40 million visit Italy—and this brings into the host countries between $30 and $45 billion. However, it takes us back to our starting point—Europe's potential future as a giant museum.

The United States, in view of its great indebtedness or for other reasons, may face a sudden major setback. It could be that the growth of China and India in view of their internal economic, social, and economic imbalances will suddenly slow or even be reversed. The rise of communist parties in India could be the harbinger of severe tensions and old-style class struggle. All this is possible, but Europe would not necessarily profit from these developments; on the contrary, they would endanger the stability Europe craves and would hurt Europe's exports. It would mean that today's giants are not as strong as sometimes believed and Europe's relative standing in the world not that weak. But all things considered, it would be cold comfort, for the misfortune of others will not bring about a triumph of Europe. Again, Europe's basic problems would persist.

But men and women do not live on bread alone, and despite a well-known saying, it is not always "the economy, stupid." Many European governments since World War Two have been reelected despite a bad economic record—and, on the contrary, some have been defeated despite their reasonable performance: Sweden in 2006 is an example. We do not really know what kind of religion or ideology generates economic growth; Max Weber could account for Western Europe and North America in modern times but not for China, Japan, or South Korea. Or, to be precise, various factors might be responsible for economic enterprise, hard work, and vision. The mood of a nation depends on a variety of motives and reasons, including imponderable ones for which no one can account with any certainty.

FIVE

Russia:
A False
Dawn?

WHEN THE SOVIET UNION DISINTEGRATED, the great majority of Europeans, West and East, took a deep breath of relief and were firmly convinced that gone were the bad old days of Communist dictatorship, of Stalinism, of repression at home and aggression abroad. Western leaders welcomed Mikhail Gorbachev when he became general secretary of the Communist Party of the Soviet Union in 1985, and after him Russian presidents Boris Yeltsin and Vladimir Putin, and expressed their ardent desire to cooperate with these leaders. Collaboration with Russia in the framework of the G8 and elsewhere came under way, not because the new Russia was such a strong country but because the Western leaders thought that it would be preferable to have Moscow in their midst rather than resentful and spiteful on the outside. It was probably the right thing to do, but it is too early to say whether the approach was successful.

It was not widely realized at the time that Russia's road to freedom would be long and arduous, measured in generations rather than years or decades, and that on this road there would be many setbacks. The Soviet system had failed, but Russia still had enormous oil and gas reserves, many nuclear bombs, and a major armament industry. It was no longer a superpower, but it was still in a position to create difficulties for Europe and the United States.

The mood has changed in Russia over the last twenty years since Gorbachev first came to power, but not always for the better. Public opinion polls carried out in 2003–2004, fifteen years after the great turning point that was the collapse of the Soviet Union, showed that the old order still had many admirers among the older and the young generation. When asked whether they would vote for Joseph Stalin if he were to run for office now, less than half (46 percent) of young Russians said that they would definitely not vote for him. Fifty-one percent said that Stalin had been a wise leader, and 56 percent thought that he had done more good than harm (*Foreign Affairs,* February 2006).

These results did not necessarily mean that there was enormous enthusiasm for the late great leader, but it did show that if there had been de-Stalinization in Russian, it had not been very thorough. "Democracy" had become a dirty word for many, a synonym for decline, corruption, decadence, anarchy, the rule of the antipatriotic forces. This mood expressed itself not only in reflections about the past but also, more importantly, in current policies and attitudes.

It is difficult to define the political character of contemporary Russia. It certainly has not become a democracy. On the contrary, the trend has been away from democratic structures toward an authoritarian regime. There are elections, but they cannot possibly be described as free and unfettered. There are political parties, but they do not have much to say. There is censorship, direct and indirect, but it is not total, compared to the censorship under communist and fascist regimes. There is no independent judiciary. Power is in the hands of the leader and the *siloviki,* the men in positions of strength, very often former (or current) officials of the secret police and their hangers-on.

In some respects, present-day Russia resembles tsarist Russia after 1905, with its nationalist official ideology, close relations with the church, and other similarities. But in other respects a post-Soviet Russia is, of course, quite different from the old monarchy.

For a while after the breakdown of the Soviet system it seemed as if Russia had opted out of world politics and even European affairs, being so preoccupied with its own domestic problems. But this situation did not last long; after a few years Russia returned as an active player, admittedly with great weaknesses but also with considerable strength, eager to restore its old sphere of influence. The mood (how could it have happened—and who was responsible for it?) was not dissimilar to that prevailing in Germany after the First World War and the Treaty of Versailles (1919), the loss of part of its territory, and its humiliation—except that in the case of Russia there had not even been a lost war, merely an implosion. It is for this reason, if for no other, that Russia cannot be ignored in any discussion about Europe's future.

Who is to blame for the developments inside Russia—or was

the growing anti-Western feeling perhaps more or less inevitable and were those in the West who hoped for democratization and peaceful coexistence simply deluding themselves? Was the Putin government perhaps the kind of regime most Russians wanted and needed?

It should have been clear since the late 1970s (indeed it was clear to some) that the Soviet system did not work well at all. Stagnation in all fields had become the norm rather than the exception, and this, very broadly speaking, was the background to Mikhail Gorbachev's rise to power. But Gorbachev, who looked to Sweden rather than the old Soviet Union for a model, labored under the delusion that the Soviet system could be radically reformed. Others in the leadership took a much harder line, and it seems in retrospect that if their coup against the "liberals" had succeeded in 1991, the old system could have lasted for another decade. As it was, Gorbachev's reforms, however well-meant, led to an acute economic crisis and a weakening of state power and ultimately to the secession of the non-Russian republics.

Gorbachev had to give way to Boris Yeltsin (ruled 1990–99), under whose leadership a chaotic privatization took place. Yeltsin seems to have had a real commitment to the democratization of the country, but he did not have much support outside of a small group of liberal intellectuals. Furthermore, he was unlucky inasmuch as the economic situation was less than auspicious (unlike his successor, Putin, he did not benefit from high oil prices), and once the initial impetus had faded, power seemed to slip out of his hands. At a time when the majority of Russians wanted above all a strong leader and a strong state, Yeltsin provided neither leadership nor stability.

The unofficial slogan of that period was *"Enrichissez-vous"* ("Get rich"), as it had been in France in the period between 1830 and 1848. People who happened to be in privileged positions in such institutions as the Communist Party, the state bureaucracy, or the KGB or had the right connections amassed enormous fortunes within a few years. The business oligarchs supported Yeltsin because they could not possibly have had a more convenient and pliable political leadership. But Yeltsin, often drunk and even more often awkward and embarrassing in his political appearances, constantly making impulsive decisions, hiring and firing new people in key positions, could not hold on to power. While it has not been proven that Yeltsin was personally more corrupt than other politicians, those around him ("the family") certainly were deeply involved in major scandals. The best Yeltsin could do was appoint his own successor, Vladimir Putin, on the understanding that neither Yeltsin nor those closest to him would be prosecuted at some future date. Seven years after his resignation, on the occasion of his seventy-fifth birthday, Yeltsin declared that Putin had been the right choice for Russia. It certainly had been the right choice for Yeltsin.

Not yet aged fifty at the time, Vladimir Putin had made his career in the KGB, having spent several years in East Germany under the old regime. His last rank was that of lieutenant colonel. He later became an aide to Anatoly Sobchak, the mayor of St. Petersburg, whom he served loyally, eventually becoming his deputy. He helped his boss even when at a later stage Sobchak ran into trouble and had to flee the country.

Putin later belonged to Yeltsin's entourage and was made head of the FSB, the successor to the KGB, which was, however, considerably weakened and could not be compared in influence to the old KGB. Putin had never pushed himself into the limelight and very little was known about him when he acceded to power. Perhaps there was not that much to know, as some of his critics said. He was not a person of strong ideological convictions one way or another, and in his election campaigns he was all things to all people.

He was certainly not a Marxist-Leninist; one would look in vain in his speeches for a quotation or an idea derived from this ideological heritage. His KGB background simply meant that he was a patriot and believed in a strong Russia. When the question of a national anthem and national symbols in general arose he opted for continuity, reintroducing the old anthem of the Stalinist period. It also meant a certain style of work: Only "our people" could be trusted, meaning those of a similar background—preferably those with whom he had worked in the past. But this was not new in Russian and Soviet history, nor has the syndrome been confined to Russia.

In crisis situations such as the disastrous sinking of the submarine *Kursk* (2000) in the Arctic Ocean or the Beslan massacre in the Caucasus in September 2004, he did not show a very sure touch. But he was favored by an improvement in the economic situation that began the very year he came to power (2000), and his campaign against the oligarchs was also quite popular. The fact that many of the early oligarchs had been of Jewish origin did not make them any more popular. But it is interesting to note that the state bureaucracy, according to most polls, was even less popular. When a member of the Russian royal family early in the nineteenth century returned to his country after a long absence, he asked his cousin the tsar, "What's new in Russia?" The tsar answered laconically, *"Nichevo, kradut"* ("Nothing, people are stealing").

The (relative) prosperity enabled the government to raise pensions, which remained, however, still very low by any standard. Average wages rose to $210 in 2004, but disparities in income were still enormous. Moscow in the early years of the new century had all the appearances of a boomtown, with many new buildings, luxury shops, and an enormous number of new cars causing major traffic jams. One-quarter of the gross domestic product came from this city and a high percentage of investments, foreign and domestic, went to the capital. The problem was that there was much less of a boom outside the capital and few investments. Moscow was booming, but the Russian countryside became depopulated, thousands of villages ceased to exist, 30 percent of the population of the Russian Far East and the Russian North had disappeared over a number of years, and the exodus from Siberia, never very densely populated, continued. Where would Russia's borders be a few decades hence?

Life was still very hard for the great majority of Russians, and those who depended on a pension—millions of them—were worse off. At the same time more than thirty billionaires had emerged, many of whom believed in ostentatious spending. Putin was not in principle opposed to the existence of some very rich people—under him the wealth of the billionaires doubled in the course of one year (2004–5). But he strongly disliked those who combined wealth with political ambitions, such as the oligarch Boris Berezovsky and media magnate Vladimir Gusinsky, who soon found themselves in exile, and the billionaire industrialist Mikhail Khodorkovsky, who ended up in a Siberian labor camp. In the contest between the oligarchs and the KGB and other state bureaucrats, it soon became clear where the power was located. Many of the big companies, especially the more profitable among them, were indirectly taken over by the state or, to be precise, by a privileged caste within the state apparatus. A new form of corporate capitalism emerged that has been compared to the state of affairs in Venezuela or Libya. The remaining oligarchs understood that they would be able to hold on to their riches only if they actively supported the Kremlin and ingratiated themselves with the officials in key positions. Of the democratic reforms under Yeltsin (such as freedom of expression), not much remained under his successor. The television and radio stations were taken over by people or companies close to the government, and as for the print media, some independent voices were left alone, but their outreach was small and they did not constitute a danger to the president and his supporters.

Unlike under Communism there was no political party acting as a transmission belt. Unity, the main group in the Duma (the Russian parliament), had been established to ensure support for Putin, but it was mainly an instrument for getting the votes in elections; it had no other function, unlike the old Communist Party. Generally speaking, there was very little active political life in the country, but such calm (which was taken for stability) was probably what most Russians wanted after the unquiet years following the collapse of the old Soviet Union. Putin's popularity, in any case, remained high throughout the two terms of his presidency (he was reelected in March 2004), and this despite the second Chechen war, which was anything but popular.

Concerning foreign policy, closer to Putin's heart than domestic and economic affairs, he steered a middle course between those who wanted to collaborate with the West and the revanchists who saw in America and the other Western countries the root of all evil. There was inside Russia a great deal of disappointment with the West; massive help, something like another Marshall Plan, had been expected but never materialized. Later on, with the steep increase in oil and gas prices, such help was no longer needed. The expansion of NATO and the European Union was considered a threat to Russian interests. America and Western Europe were also accused of helping the independent forces in republics such as Ukraine and Georgia, which had seceded from the Soviet Union and which the Kremlin considered hostile. Protracted negotiations with the European Union proved inconclusive. True, Washington and the European capitals frequently talked about a partnership with Russia and there were all kinds of political steps to establish closer relations. Democratic reforms in Russia were loudly welcomed, even at a time when it should have been clear that Russia was moving away from democratization and that Russia was on the way to becoming an autocratic state.

Putin realized, however, that Russia shared some common interests with Washington and Europe, for instance in combating terrorism, and he thought it foolish to enter on a collision course with the West as the ultranationalists at home wanted.

But Russia wanted not only recognition and respect, it also wanted to regain as much as possible of its old sphere of influence, and therefore conflict was bound to arise. It might have been more sensible to proceed more slowly with such a policy. But Putin and his colleagues probably felt various kinds of pressure—political pressure to show results, as well as economic pressure—the oil weapon was formidable, but who could know how long it would last? Above all, there was demographic pressure: The population of Russia was steadily declining, and once the population of Russia fell below a certain limit, the imperial dreams would be over. According to UN projections, the population of Russia in 2050 will be between 70 and 100 million. According to other UN projections, the population of Pakistan will double by 2020. But of Russia's population at least a quarter, probably more, will not be ethnic Russians, and the population will be aged. Will this be sufficient to keep the enormous landmass from Kaliningrad in the west to Vladivostok in the east—not to mention the realization of imperial ambitions? About 30 percent of the population of the Russian Far East has disappeared during the last decade, about two-thirds from the Russian North. The Russian exodus from Siberia continues.

RUSSIA HAS BECOME A VERY important supplier of oil and gas for Western Europe, especially to Germany and Italy and to a smaller extent to Britain and France. This dependence with regard to energy could turn into political dependence; in an article in a professional journal of small circulation, Putin pointed out well before he became president that oil and gas supplies were the most important instrument to regain great power status. The Russian threats to increase prices or turn off the supply altogether (as it did, briefly, with Ukraine and Georgia) were warning signs.

It was obvious that Russia would not lose its interest in Ukraine; old Kiev after all was the cradle of Russian statehood, and many millions of ethnic Russians live in Eastern Ukraine. The Baltic countries were probably lost despite the presence of a significant number of Russians living there, but these were small and unimportant. By 2006, however, Russia had not given up on Moldova (or, to be precise, the breakaway Russian-speaking region Transnistria), and it had its military presence (under the guise of peacekeeping) in South Ossetia and Abkhazia as well as in Ingushetia, which was ruled by a FSB (KGB) general, which could be used against Georgia. The populations of these breakaway regions have been granted Russian citizenship. In Central Asia, Russia's position has been strengthened because of the weakness of the national governments, which, largely unpopular at home, depended on various kinds of Russian help, economic, political, and military.

The Caucasus confronted Moscow with the most difficult problems. Chechen separatism was a wound that would not heal, and there was the danger that the infection would spread; it was no longer certain to what extent Daghestan, the republic to the north of Chechnya, was under Russian control. It seems clear in retrospect that the Chechnya situation could have been handled more wisely by Moscow; greater inducements could have been offered to the Chechens to remain, if not part of Russia, then very closely connected with it. Russia was afraid that it might lose the whole Caucasus if it made concessions that were too far-reaching.

Major military operations in the second Chechen war ended in 2002, but order has not been restored in this region. While Chechnya was largely destroyed, the price that Russia had to pay was high: Several thousand soldiers were killed and many more wounded; the war had a negative impact on the Russian armed forces, let Russian capacity to lead a guerrilla war appear in a bad light, and harmed Russia politically. While Chechen resistance had been originally tribal-nationalist, as the fighting continued the resistance became more radical, Islamist-jihadist as well as nationalist. There was the danger that terrorism would spread in the Caucasus and eventually (as the leaders of the Chechen rebellion threatened) would involve other parts of the country.

Russia attempted with some success to establish closer relations with Turkey, Iran, and Arab countries, partly no doubt in order to prevent the internationalization of the Caucasian conflict— assuming that these countries, in recognition of the political and technological help they received from Moscow, would refrain from backing radical Muslims inside Russia. It was by no means clear, however, whether such gratitude could be expected in the long run. Furthermore, such a policy, which included providing arms to neighbors on whose goodwill they could not count forever, could have dangerous repercussions concerning Russia's long-term interests. This policy had been advocated well before Putin by Foreign Minister Yevgeny Primakov, a former head of the KGB and also a prime minister, and it was bound to complicate Russian relations with the West.

It is frequently forgotten that some 15 to 20 million Muslims live in Russia; their exact number is unknown, but their birthrate is certainly considerably higher than the Russian (1.2 at present). In addition, the number of "guest workers" from the Central Asian republics in Russia could well amount by now to a few million. Projections according to which Muslims will outnumber Russians within a generation are almost certainly exaggerated. There has been a strong movement toward full autonomy in the regions densely settled by Muslims, such as Tatarstan, and it will probably gain momentum.

Separatism is unlikely because Russian Muslims are not living in a contiguous region but are dispersed widely over European Russia—Tatarstan, Bashkortostan, Crimea, the Caucasus—at least a million Muslims live in Moscow. (According to some estimates, the figure for the Moscow conurbation is far higher.) Official statistics say that some 20 million foreign citizens were entering Russia for work in 2005. Most of them came apparently from neighboring republics, especially from Central Asia; this high figure probably referred to multiple entries. Even in the autonomous republics such as Tatarstan (52 percent) and Bashkortostan (55 percent), Muslim majorities are not great. But radical Islamists have been active in these concentrations, legally and more often illegally, and political tensions are likely to increase especially in view of the growing xenophobia ("Russia for the Russians") among the ethnic Russians.

The danger of a neofascist or national Bolshevik coup was

exaggerated at the time of the breakdown of the Soviet Union. At present the odds are against it precisely because the Putin government cannot easily be outflanked in displays of patriotism. But potentially the danger continues to exist. The Communists under Gennady Zyuganov are still the second largest force in the Duma, and the neofascists, while still relatively small in numbers, are now better organized than ten or fifteen years ago.

The influence of the Communists has declined somewhat: They lost seats in the elections of 1999, and in 2004 they did not even seriously compete, being aware that Putin's victory was assured. At a time when the majority of the Russian people live in misery, however, and when thousands of villages simply disappear following a mass escape from the countryside, there is a reservoir for a party of the poor even under the uninspired leadership of Zyuganov, a person wholly lacking in charisma.

It is difficult to point to any specific communist content in the ideology of this movement, except that they oppose liberalization and privatization of the economy. Of old-style Marxism-Leninism little has remained; and of proletarian internationalism, nothing. The Communists are as nationalist as the far right. They are the party of the "true Russians"; for alien elements (which includes about everyone not of Russian extraction) there is room neither in their ranks nor in the country, unless they make themselves as inconspicuous as possible.

If the Communists are more or less united, the extreme right and neofascist groups, while very active and loud, are divided into many sects and factions. Moreover, it is not at all easy to establish with any certainty which of them are bona fide superpatriots and fascists and which are sponsored or assisted by the FSB (KGB). As in the last decades of tsarist rule, the secret police infiltrated these groups and, to a certain extent, took a hand in their operations. On occasion these groups supported by the police escaped the secret tutelage; this happened in the period before 1914 and it could happen now.

The leading groups of the Russian radical right all originate one way or another from Pamyat, a group that first appeared during the last years of Soviet power. However, while Pamyat was basically in the ideological tradition of the prerevolutionary Russian far right (anti-Semitic, anti-Masonic, believing in all kinds of conspiracies, and identifying with the more reactionary trends in the Russian Orthodox Church), its successors adopted all kinds of strange and often foreign doctrines. Thousands of young fascists paraded in Moscow on November 4, 2005, shouting "Heil Hitler" and "Sieg Heil"; their gurus claimed that only fascism and Nazism offered a way out of Russia's current misery: corruption, poverty, the domination of foreigners, and general humiliation and despair.

Some tried to combine fascism and old-style communism, while others peddled all kind of religious-sectarian ideas, frequently of Far Eastern origin, astrology, various "occult sciences," and ideas often found in New Age circles in the West. Quite influential were the Eurasians; this school of thought went back to a political doctrine first developed in Prague and Paris by Russian émigrés, who preached that Russia's future was in the East rather than in the West. In its contemporary form, Eurasianism meant extreme hostility to America, which was believed to be the source of all evil, and an aggressive Russian foreign policy aiming at Russian domination of Europe and, if possible, also part of Asia. But how would it be possible to combine an alliance with Islam with deep-seated Russian xenophobia?

The problem was, of course, that the "Asianism" these ideologues invoked existed only in their imagination. As far as China and Japan were concerned, they had no wish to enter into a close alliance with Russia; on the contrary, they constituted a threat to Russia in Asia in view of their great numerical strength. As for the world of Islam, Russian relations had never been close, and the idea of establishing a Russian-Turkish or Russian-Iranian or Russian-Arab axis seemed far-fetched in an age in which "Russia for the Russians" was the chief slogan of the Russian right (according to polls, more than 50 percent of all Russians agreed with this slogan) and jihadism had many supporters in the Muslim world. This idea may appeal to some political leaders, but it is deeply unpopular among the masses. Such an alliance was impracticable unless, of course, the Eurasians envisioned Russia as a junior partner, which they most certainly did not.

Some of the leaders of these sects (which often split, changed their names, and reunited) were colorful characters. Aleksander Dugin managed to produce an ideology consisting of the most diverse, incoherent, and contradictory elements of European radical thinking of the extreme left and right, as well as astrology and other occult sciences. He also succeeded in persuading the Soviet army general staff that the doctrine he preached was the best—nay, the only—way to restore the patriotic spirit among young Russians. Eduard Limonov was a writer and entertainer who went into politics. He accused Dugin, with whom he had originally collaborated, of being too closely connected with the political-military establishment and split with him.

Limonov's group, the National Bolshevik Party, was outlawed for a while, as was Alexander Barkashov's Russian National Unity, with its paramilitary units called Russian knights. But on the whole, these groups have not been under strong pressure from the security forces, which regarded them as basically harmless young people who were occasionally excessive in their youthful vigor. Most prominent and active in the streets have been the Russian skinheads who celebrate Hitler's birthday each year. There seems to have been a nonaggression pact between them and the security forces, which interfere only on occasions when one or more foreigners are killed in the streets.

The gurus of the extreme right groups such as Dugin, who were considered, at best, eccentrics in the nineties and not taken seriously by anyone, have become quite fashionable among sections of the intelligentsia and are frequently interviewed in journals that were once the strongholds of the liberal intelligentsia.

And yet, with all this, it is difficult to envisage a great future for neofascism in Russia, unless of course a total breakdown should take place. Openly attacking the current political establishment would not be too popular, and the attacks against Caucasian fruit and vegetable dealers in Moscow markets do not amount to a major policy campaign. Most Jews have left Russia, and those who remain are no longer the great demonic enemy. The neo-Nazis generate a paroxysm of hatred against America, which they believe brought about the downfall of their country. But America is distant, and the dangers facing Russia today emanate from other, nearer quarters; there is no danger that the United States will take over the Caucasus, Siberia, or the Russian Far East.

The new Russia has great fossil fuel reserves and an impressive number of atomic weapons. But this is not a sufficient base for a return to superpower status. According to the polls, a majority of Russians would like to regain such status—Russia, after all, had been a great power for three hundred years. But when asked whether they were willing and able to make the effort needed to become again a power of this kind, the answer is far more reluctant, according to the political analyst Lilia Shevtsova. The country is still too weak for major adventures. Its economy depends on the export of raw materials rather than on the performance of its industry. It is lagging behind in modern technologies. The social ills—alcoholism, drugs, AIDS—are rampant. There may be hatred and envy of foreign and domestic enemies, but morale is not high and corruption is well above what has been considered more or less normal in the past. In brief, the country has not regained the self-confidence needed for great-power status. Such a recovery may still take a long time, and it is not certain how many Russians will be left by then.

It took the Russian leadership a long time to become aware of their demographic problem—perhaps because from their vantage point in Moscow (one giant traffic jam by the year 2000) it was easy to ignore the fact that the rest of the country was getting depopulated. There had been warning voices for a long time, but as noted in a conference arranged by the Russian parliament in March 2006, the government had not paid attention. As former foreign minister Yevgeny Primakov said on this occasion, if current trends continued, Russia would cease to exist by the middle of this century and the depopulation of Siberia and the Far East would create a vacuum and would be taken over by others even earlier without a shot being fired. Putin, in a more restrained vein, predicted in June 2006 that if current trends continued, the population of Russia by the end of the century would be half of what it is today. The population decline was an issue of the highest priority for national security. If there still was a "Russian Idea," it was how to save the country from extinction. But the ministers of defense and the generals had never gone to the meetings where these problems had been discussed. Who did they think would defend the homeland fifteen or twenty years hence?—assuming, as one member interjected, there was still a homeland to be defended.

The Putin government issued a decree in May 2006 providing for a monthly support of $55 for the first child and $110 for a second child born. More important, mothers should be given a one-time award of several thousand dollars, a considerable sum by Russian standards. Altogether, the Russian government allocated 30 to 40 billion rubles to promote an increase in the birthrate. But a high percentage of Russian women still did not want to have children. Further, it was not clear who exactly would make these payments—the state or local authorities—and there had been reports in the past about abuses of such schemes, such as passing on children to orphanages after having pocketed the award. If the initiative succeeded, it would be the first time in history that financial awards would cause a lasting increase in the birthrate.

SIX

The Failure
of Integration,
and Europe's
Future

What Went Wrong?

A WRITER IN *The Economist* recently complained about conventional
wisdom considering contemporary Europe a washed-up, aging,
economically stagnant continent destined inexorably to lose
ground not only to a dynamic United States but also to China and
even India. But this was not the conventional wisdom on the campuses and in the think tanks of the United States until recently,

and even in Europe there have been speeches, books, and official declarations replete with optimism. As these lines are written the German economy is doing better than in recent years, so perhaps the doomsayers were wrong after all. But the improvement could well be temporary or a mirage leading to renewed pessimism on the markets and stock exchanges.

Conventional opinion, however, like conventional medicine, is not always wrong, nor is the phenomenon of rise and decline in any way unprecedented. History is woven of the rise and decline of countries and civilizations and the waxing and waning of great powers: not one has lasted forever, and some have disappeared. They have declined for a great variety of reasons, some for economic causes, others because they were defeated in war, some because over time they were exhausted and lost their will or spiritual strength and no longer cared whether they reproduced themselves. Gibbon wrote that the ancient Greeks thought that Rome prevailed over their country because of "fortune," that is to say, mere accident. It was at least in part by accident that the eastern Roman empire lasted for a thousand years after the western part had disappeared.

The question of why nations have declined can be discussed endlessly. When the story of the decline of Europe in the twentieth century comes to be written, it may well be asked not why the continent's power diminished but why European dominance lasted so long. Migration may have played a certain role in the decline of nations, but by itself migration has as often strengthened as weakened nations. Both medieval and modern history are histories of migrations: One should think only of European migration to North and South America (Italian and Spanish), of the Huguenots migrating to Germany and other European countries, of the Polish migration to France and Germany in the twentieth century, of the Russian immigration to France after 1917, of the Jewish emigration from Eastern Europe, and of Chinese and Indian immigrants establishing major communities in Southeast Asia and even Africa. Very often these were the more enterprising elements who left their native countries for whatever reasons and both sides benefited: The immigrants worked their way up in society and the countries that absorbed them profited from the newcomers' skills and talents. Strong, self-confident societies have almost always been able to absorb such waves of immigrants and to make the best of it. There always were initial difficulties; even in a country of immigrants such as the United States, for a long time neither the Irish nor the Jews, let alone the "yellow peril," were welcome. Sometimes the new immigrants found it difficult to accept the laws and the way of life of the new countries; some, for instance, refused to serve in the military. There was almost always a certain return migration, but the majority remained in what became their new homes and after a few generations they became part and parcel of it.

This is true also for our time. I have already discussed the contributions made by the Indian immigration to Britain, the Chinese to the United States and other parts of the world, the Sikhs and the Armenians, the Cypriots, and a considerable variety of other people. Polish guest workers are welcome all over Europe and Filipinos all over the world. True, in an age of aggressive nationalism, ethnic minorities found themselves under pressure: Idi Amin threw the Indians out of Uganda; Gamal Abdel Nasser expelled Greeks, Italians, and other Europeans as well as the Jews from Egypt, even if they had lived there for generations. The Chinese minorities found themselves under pressure in Southeast Asia. These were relatively small groups, and it was only in Europe that the issue of Muslim immigrants became a major political problem. Integration did not work, partly because it was not wanted by the newcomers. Multiculturalism led to the emergence of parallel societies and had frequently negative consequences.

Inevitably, this led to soul-searching: Whose fault was it, and what could be done to remedy it? One of the reasons was, of course, that the countries of Europe were not accustomed to absorbing millions of foreigners rooted in wholly different cultures, who had no particular desire to give up their old ways of life and accept the customs of their new home countries. This is not a specific European feature; it can be found all over the world, excepting only countries that depended largely through long periods of their history on a flow of immigrants, such as the nations of North America, some Latin American countries, Canada, and Australia. Elsewhere, dislike of foreigners, even of those close in language, religion, and culture, has been deeply rooted and widespread. Even the fate of the Palestinian refugees in the Arab countries has often been an unhappy one—they were frequently kept in camps, sometimes expelled, and only rarely given citizenship, even though there was no dearth of speeches that stressed solidarity with these persecuted brothers and sisters.

But there were other reasons as well. To begin with, Muslim immigration to Europe was largely unplanned and uncontrolled. It continued a long time even after it should have been clear that the "guest workers" had no wish to return to their countries of origin, and long after it appeared that there was no work for them. To a certain extent this immigration was a consequence of the imperial past—Algerians had a right to settle in France; and West Indians and Indians expelled from Uganda, in Britain. But this postcolonial explanation did not extend to others, the majority, who had been born long after the imperial power had given up its former possessions and these countries had gained independence. And it did not apply at all to those who went to Germany or Sweden, to Austria, the Netherlands, or Belgium.

There was and to a certain extent still is a self-blaming school of thought in some European countries according to which the failure of integration was the fault of European societies, which had not shown sufficient goodwill toward the immigrants and had not invested enough funds in helping with their housing and in other respects, including education. But European societies—individual citizens—had never been asked whether they wanted millions of new neighbors in their country; these citizens had the right to vote on all kind of issues, domestic and foreign, but about this very essential issue no one had ever consulted them. Governments and corporations had initiated it. Would they have acted differently had they foreseen the consequences of their policy?

Even this question cannot be answered with certainty. Some might have been more cautious concerning immigration and granting the right of asylum. Others might not have cared, believing that their countries (and Europe in general) had no particular contribution to make anymore, that they had more or less fulfilled their historical mission (if there ever had been one), and that maintaining their social and cultural identity was not a matter of paramount importance in the modern world. With the nations suffering from exhaustion, perhaps the time had come to hand over the torch of civilization to other people, religions, and ethnic groups.

In some cases, such as in Scandinavia and in the Netherlands, a bad conscience dating back to the 1930s, when refugees from Nazi Germany were in most cases refused asylum even though they were racially or politically persecuted, might have played a role. In Germany, too, there was the fear of being accused of racism if they rejected immigrants. It is difficult even in retrospect to establish what the authorities in these countries were thinking. Did they imagine that uncontrolled immigration would not involve major problems; that the economic, social, and cultural problems would be solved; and that the immigrants would one day disappear or that they would be well integrated?

All this is not to say that self-confident European societies should have closed their gates hermetically against all immigrants. But they should have been directed to productive labor rather than to being recipients of welfare services from the day of their arrival. Preachers and agitators inciting their fold against the decadent and sinful Western way of life should have been expelled. They should have been expected to behave in accordance with the law of the land and the values and prevailing norms. If these laws and norms were not according to their convictions, they would have been free to leave. This, after all, had been the case all throughout history. Christians from Central Europe and Jews from Eastern Europe had gone to America precisely because they felt discriminated against or persecuted.

However, the European governments and societies were no longer self-confident; xenophobia had not disappeared, but among the establishment little pride was left of belonging to a certain nation (or to Europe); a cultural and moral relativism had prevailed, partly perhaps in reaction to an exaggerated nationalism of past ages. Such societies were not in a position to provide guidance to newcomers but were highly permissive. Newcomers to these countries were bound to gain the impression that prevailing laws and norms could safely be ignored.

These attitudes, coupled with cultural and moral relativism, were bound to have far-reaching consequences, and European societies will have to live with them. Illegal immigrants to Japan or China, Singapore, or virtually any other country would have been sent back within days, if not hours, to their countries of origin. The United States faced a similar problem with Mexican immigrants, but at least they did not want to impose a new and foreign religious law upon the country they moved into. Illegal immigrants to Europe were permitted to stay. But even if the authorities had taken a harsher course, this would have affected only a minority, since most members of the immigrant communities are by now citizens of their countries of adoption or were born there and have as much right to live there as everyone else.

It is now gradually being realized how this will affect Europe's future—combined with the other threats facing the continent. It certainly means the end of Europe as a major player in world affairs. As has been mentioned, misfortunes could befall other continents, too. A great number of cosmic disasters could happen elsewhere. Some have been described in works of science fiction, others are listed and discussed in a recent work by Richard A. Posner (*Catastrophe: Risk and Response*, 2004). They range from bioterrorism, a pandemic, and global warming to a collision with a comet. But chances are that in such cases of worldwide catastrophe Europe, too would be affected, so it wouldn't be an occasion for schadenfreude.

The Chinese economic megaboom may come to an end as the result of the weaknesses of crony capitalism and the weakness of the political infrastructure, as well as the public health and educational system, or state opposition to political reform could lead to the alienation of the masses. The Indian boom may come to a sudden end. Only a fraction of the population has benefited from the prosperity; the boom is leading to enormous disparities between rich and poor, between cities and countryside, and it could lead to political conflict. The enormous economic power of the United States rests on uncertain foundations, beginning with the massive national debt and trade deficits. There could be foreign political setbacks and a growth of domestic tensions.

All these disasters might happen, but they would not benefit Europe. The European economy is largely export oriented, and as the domestic market is shrinking, the economy will be even more export oriented in future. Setbacks affecting its major markets would almost certainly cause a crisis in Europe.

To repeat, uncontrolled immigration was not the only reason for the decline of Europe. But taken together with the continent's other misfortunes, it led to a profound crisis; a miracle might be needed to extract Europe from these predicaments.

Europe: What Remains?

NO ONE CAN say with any certainty whether European unification will make much progress in the years to come or how the European economy will perform. But the demographic problems can be foreseen with a reasonable degree of accuracy, and it is to these that we shall turn first. True, even population projections are based on certain assumptions, and as the French demographer Jean-Claude Chesnais has noted, projections made by bodies like the United Nations very often err on the side of political correctness and optimism, as they do not want to shock and they downplay political implications. Estimates by individual experts are often more reliable.

However, even the UN projections that are based on the assumption that Europe's birthrate will rise by about one-quarter in the years to come (which most think unrealistic) have concluded that by the year 2050 the old European Union will have 60 million fewer inhabitants and the whole of Europe (Russia included) will be diminished by 130 million. More important yet, after 2050 population decline will be far more rapid because by that time the average age will be much higher and the number of births in a country like Germany will be only half that of today. If one omits from view further immigration into Europe—and there is every reason that immigration will be smaller for political as well as economic reasons (e.g., unemployment)—countries with a low birthrate such as Italy and Spain will have shrunk substantially, as pointed out in some detail earlier on.

Such shrinking of the population can be observed even now in parts of Europe, as in European Russia, where thousands of villages have ceased to exist (not to mention the exodus from Siberia and other parts of northern Russia). In Spain the rural depopulation began in the post-Franco era; it also affected Andalusia and very poor regions such as Extremadura and has gathered speed in recent years. It has been attempted without much success to resettle new immigrants in deserted villages. There is a sizable Latin American immigration (especially from Ecuador and Colombia) to Spain, but these newcomers usually move to the cities where the better-paid jobs are.

In Britain, Manchester and Newcastle have lost 20 percent of their population in the last forty years. About 100,000 people leave London each year. While London house prices are still astronomical even compared with those in the United States and on the Continent, houses can be bought for next to nothing in the inner cities in the Midlands and the North, where the old, traditional industries have disappeared. It is particularly in these parts that strong Muslim communities exist.

In Germany depopulation is particularly strong in the eastern part of the country where the younger people have left. Two thousand schools have closed down in recent years, there are few shops left and even fewer doctors, and it seems only a question of time before the last ones in many villages also leave. But the shrinkage is not limited to the countryside. The number of inhabitants in small towns and some bigger ones is also rapidly falling, the prices of houses have gone down, and even deserted streets can be seen here and there. Halle and Rostock, Cottbus, and Magdeburg lost 16 to 20 percent of their inhabitants during the last decade—most of the young generation.

Düsseldorf, which has also lost inhabitants, is still the major banking and trade center of the region, but the Ruhr, Germany's rust belt, is steadily declining, and nearby cities, including Hagen, have lost many of their inhabitants. The fate of Hagen or Gelsenkirchen is more typical of the whole area than that of Düsseldorf, and the same goes for the steel and mining regions of southern Belgium (Charleroi and Mons, for instance) and also the cities in France across the Belgian border. The ethnic tensions in Antwerp (Anvers), once a peaceful and prosperous city, have made it one of the most problematic cities in Western Europe. There are sections of cities in which few children can be seen; these cities resemble more old people's homes and no longer correspond with our traditional image of vibrant, pulsating city life.

But who will take care of this aging population, and who will be the young, productive workers in the economy who ensure the economic health of the country so that pensions to the elderly can be provided as well as the funds for health and other services? At one time, it was believed that Eastern Europe could provide this labor force, but the number of those who came was small and it is going to dry up even more because birthrates in Eastern Europe are as low as (or even lower than) in Western Europe.

There is a great and growing reservoir of young unemployed

in North Africa and the Middle East—about 25 percent—and population growth is outpacing economic growth. A hundred million jobs will be needed for the next ten years to solve the problem, but they are unlikely to be created. The unemployment issue in North Africa and the Arab East has been called a time bomb, and the question arises whether it will explode in the Middle East or in Europe or in both regions.

But aside from political considerations, what would be the point of inviting people from these parts at a time when unemployment among young people from Muslim countries is 20 percent, 30 percent, even 40 percent in Germany, France, and other European countries? To have more young workers who are not only unskilled but sometimes also lacking drive and motivation would aggravate current ethnic tensions but not help to meet the economic and social needs.

South Asia, Southeast Asia, and the former Soviet Central Asian republics could be a more promising source of labor. But so far the countries of Europe have made little effort to attract emigrants from these parts, nor is it certain how many skilled workers and technicians would be willing to move to Europe at a time when the economy in their own countries is picking up. In Germany for a short time attempts were made to attract computer experts from Bangalore and other centers of the Indian high-tech industry. But the offers made were not very attractive and there were few candidates. (Only 20,000 German green cards were allocated to India, but few candidates showed interest and after a couple of years the scheme was stopped.) In Spain there is a renewed interest in emigrants from Latin America; tens of thousands have come in recent years, especially from Ecuador and Colombia, and the question arose whether this movement should be expanded.

How likely is a rise in the birthrate in the European societies? The birthrate has been falling for the last 150 years and a reversal seems unlikely now. The dictatorships of the 1930s and the Soviet Union tried by various premiums and rewards to pursue natalist policies, but without significant success. It has been suggested in Russia that members of families with children should be given preference in state employment. In France and Sweden family-friendly legislation (providing for long holidays connected with childbirth) have probably caused a slight increase in the birthrate, and it seems likely that other countries may follow their example. But in France and Sweden the birthrate remains well below the reproduction rate. In brief, short of developments that cannot be foreseen, the prevailing trend will not be reversed.

True, the Chinese and Japanese (and of late also the Indian) birthrates have also significantly decreased, and the same is likely to happen eventually in the Middle East and North Africa. It seems equally certain that the birthrate of the immigrant communities in Europe, at present significantly higher than that of the local population (perhaps three times as high), will also decline. But the impact of this decline will be palpably felt only in a generation or two and will not be felt during the next decades.

The Future of Muslim Europe: United Kingdom

THE IMMIGRANT COMMUNITIES in Europe differ greatly in many respects, and the problems that will face European societies in the years to come will differ, too. Generalizations about Muslim communities are of use only up to a point.

The essential facts about immigrants to the United Kingdom from Muslim countries have been noted earlier: They constitute only about half of the total (1.6 million—perhaps somewhat more, counting the illegals); about half are British-born. It is a young community and their birthrate is fairly high. Unemployment among young Muslims is three times higher than among the general public. Most observers have noted not only cultural alienation but also a growing feeling of discrimination and disaffection in their midst.

Thus a reservoir for violent action does exist, as the arrest of Pakistani "militants" in August 2006 has shown. But politically Muslims in Britain will not be a decisive force on the national level in the foreseeable future, unless the British government permits uncontrolled immigration in the years to come, which is unlikely in view of past experience. British Muslims will take a larger and more active part in political life on the local level as municipal counselors and even mayors of cities (such as Mohammed Afzal Khan in Manchester) and also as members of Parliament. Muslims will hardly be a decisive political force except perhaps in inner-city wards of places like Bradford and Birmingham and in some sections of London, perhaps forty to fifty constituencies altogether, such as Birmingham-Sparkbrook, Bethnal Green, and East Ham. Politicians in these regions pay closer attention to the Muslim vote; given the British electoral system, the outcome in a few dozen constituencies could still be of importance. Dozens of British members of Parliament will have to look over their shoulders to see whether their attitude on Kashmir, Palestine/Israel, and such has been sufficiently politically correct. The Muslims may want to establish an ethnic party, but this is not very likely. Coalitions with other ethnic or religious groups are possible, but it is doubtful that they will last.

The British government has tried harder than any other European government to accommodate their Muslim communities—on the macro level by permitting almost indiscriminately Muslim immigration and the activities of extremist groups outlawed in the Arab world. As mentioned earlier, in the 1990s London became the center of Islamist radical activities. At the same time, great efforts have been undertaken to enter a dialogue with Muslim organizations—and not only the moderates among them—working groups have been established to reduce disaffection, and laws have been passed to protect Muslim interests and prevent discrimination. On the micro level, preferential treatment has been given to Muslim immigrants for housing and other social services. Some of these efforts were laudable, but the results were meager. According to a massive study of attitudes carried out by the Pew Foundation in June 2006, on the one hand some 63 percent of Britons took a favorable view of the Muslim minority in their country, but on the other hand British Muslims had "a much more negative view of Westerners than [did] Muslim minorities in Germany, France or Spain," charging Britons with such negative characteristics as selfishness, arrogance, violence, greed, immorality, and fanaticism. British Muslims were also more prone to believe in conspiracy theories; only 17 percent of them accepted that the terrorist attacks of September 11, 2001, had been carried out by Arabs—in contrast, for instance, to 48 percent of French Muslims. If relations between the ethnic groups were bad, more Britons tended to blame their own people than Muslims (which, if correct, tends to show that the complaints about Islamophobia are largely bogus), whereas the Muslims blamed the Britons.

Many more British than other European Muslims (47 percent) were pessimistic about the future inasmuch as there was a conflict between being a devout Muslim and living in a modern democratic society. According to the same poll, German and Spanish citizens expressed considerably more negative opinions about Muslims living in their country than did the British; Indian attitudes toward Muslims (and also Nigerian attitudes), however, were much more critical than any of the Europeans.

Not every region in Britain has been closely investigated, but there are such studies concerning London's East End (Tower Hamlets, formerly known as Bethnal Green, Wapping, Bow, Stepney, and Poplar) and Bradford, and the findings have not been encouraging. A report on the New East End by Professor Geoff Dench and others is of particular interest; it is a sequel to a similar study in 1954 carried out by members of the Labour Party. Their conclusion in 2006 was that the East End is still the backside (not to use an earthier expression) of the British capital. A culture of entitlement among the immigrants has emerged and a new social order has benefited them, which has antagonized the working-class whites who felt themselves progressively disenfranchised. The conclusion: "An approach concentrating on minorities alone is adding fuel to the fire."

Once this was the East End of street markets and Jack the Ripper, of Bloom's restaurant (*lockshen* and gefilte fish), of *Dixon of Dock Green*, the legendary heartwarming television program of the 1950s, and of *Underneath the Arches*. But there was a population transfer and shift in power in the East End, which is now predominantly inhabited by Bangladeshis. This manifested itself in, among other things, crime statistics. Whereas up to the late 1990s the majority of complaints to the police about racial attacks came from new immigrants, they now come from whites, even though there has been a flight of whites from the area. However, those Bangladeshis who were economically and socially successful (mainly in restaurants and the catering business) also left the area, distancing themselves from the old ghettos, moving to cleaner and safer streets and quarters with better schools. At the same time, those who did not make it (the majority) of the young Bangladeshi men "responded to failure by adopting aspects of British counter-culture that have nothing in common with the life style of their parents." This is a polite way of referring to street gangs, gang culture, drug abuse, theft, and robbery. The reference to British counterculture seems not quite appropriate in this context. There were white criminal and semicriminal gangs roaming these streets in the years before and after the Second World War, but they have almost entirely disappeared, and they were hardly ever "counterculture." The older generation of immigrants, in any case, had hardly any control over the young among them, a situation similar to the one prevailing in France and Germany.

One important reason for white demoralization has been the educational practices in the East End. Local schools have received special allocations for helping Bangladeshi schoolchildren (under a regulation called Section 11), and this has created the impression among white parents that it has become the priority of teachers to fail white children so that the school will be seen as doing their jobs helping the minorities—and getting more allocations.

Another issue that has created a lot of tension is the preference given to new immigrants for housing, which created among the white residents a feeling of a foreign invasion. An old-timer complained about the signs in Urdu that suddenly appeared in public places such as hospitals ("This used to be a Jewish neighborhood, but I do not remember any signs in Hebrew letters"). The Bangladeshi community became more and more dependent on the welfare system, even though initially they had been reluctant to accept these handouts, which were considered in violation of their religion. Needless to say, reliance on benefits prolonged and perpetuated their inferior status in society.

The philosophy behind the policy of positive discrimination on the part of the Labour Party (the ruling party in the East End) was formulated by the chairman of the parliamentary Labour Party: that the white working class and especially the older generation among them were conservative, often incurably racist and reactionary, and that it was therefore a waste of time to spend funds and efforts on maintaining their goodwill. The Bangladeshis' higher birthrate was an additional factor of importance. However, in the elections of 2005 the Labour Party candidate, a woman of part black, part Jewish extraction, was defeated by George Galloway, the president of a new party named Respect who is widely considered a clown and a disreputable character. His movement was based on a coalition between the Trotskyite Socialist Workers Party and various radical Islamist groups. The Labour Party did not benefit from its policy; there is little gratitude in politics.

Another example is offered by Bradford, a city of about 470,000 in Lancashire, with an old Muslim community, predominantly Pakistani. There are now about 80,000 Pakistanis in Bradford, half of them born in the United Kingdom. According to a semiofficial report, there was a liberal accommodation of Muslim rights in Bradford (including granting them single-sex schools). In 1982 there was one mosque; now there are more than sixty. But it soon appeared (according to the same report) that there was no single definition of "shared values," which had always been invoked in the city.

The local authorities and the Muslim leaders had effectively turned a blind eye to the necessity of engaging in a critical dialogue about the idea of an integrated multiethnic society in the city. According to another report, Bradford became self-segregated, a city fragmented along cultural, ethnic, religious, and social lines. There were high levels of unemployment and a serious crime problem, and drugs were openly sold in the inner parts of the city.

In brief, the picture was quite similar to that of many other British cities with such an ethnic composition. Bradford was one of the places where Salman Rushdie's books were burned following the uproar over *The Satanic Verses* (published in 1989) and there were riots in 1995 and on subsequent occasions. Non-Muslims, British and Indians alike, were squeezed out (the term "ethnic cleansing" was used by some residents) as an Islamization of space took place. Churches and pubs were attacked. Non-Muslim women could not venture out in the street in the dark, and even in daytime there was a danger of being molested. In the words of letters to the local newspapers, the inner city had become a war zone. Pakistanis did take a part in local politics; there were thirteen counselors and one of them became mayor. But it was also reported that the votes of the Muslim counselors almost invariably depended on instructions given by phone from Pakistan, apparently by religious or political dignitaries.

According to a Muslim intellectual who grew up in Bradford, the local leaders of the Labour Party and those further left were at least partly responsible for these developments. They had set up a conservative local Council of Mosques and looked at it as the voice of the community:

> Multiculturalism did not create militant Islam, but it
> created a space for it within British Muslim
> communities that had not existed before. It fostered a
> more tribal nation, undermined progressive trends
> within the Muslim communities and strengthened the
> hand of the conservative religious leaders.*

Those further to the left gave up on the old Marxist idea of the working class as the agent of change and put their support be-

*Kenan Malik, "Born in Bradford," *Prospect*, October 2005.

hind all kinds of "new social movements." When this did not work very well, they supported "identity politics." In other words, what mattered was not common values but what various ethnic or tribal groups, however reactionary, demanded. Ironically, the support given to the conservative Muslim leaders, not only in Bradford but virtually all over Britain, did not pay political dividends, either. There was a growing generational conflict in the community, and the influence the religious leaders had over the young generation was small or nonexistent.

Local Muslim spokesmen did not deny the existence of serious problems but put the blame on the identity crisis from which young Muslims suffered, unemployment, lack of educational opportunities, social alienation, and Islamophobia (racism), including the "Islamophobic messages of the mass media." But according to British law, any such messages are punishable by law. In truth, there was no lack of educational opportunities. Bradford even has a university; young Pakistanis did not avail themselves of these opportunities, however—very often they did not even attend school.

An Indian journalist provided an interesting report comparing the developments of the Indian community in Leicester and the Pakistanis in Bradford. (Leicester, a city in the eastern Midlands with 330,000 inhabitants, also has a big Asian community but has been doing much better than Bradford.) The Indians, on the one hand, being the majority in Leicester, had bettered themselves. The young Pakistanis, on the other hand, had opted for empty gestures of defiance and victimhood: they wanted respect, tried to escape their miserable status by retreating into a hostile inner world, and often turned to violence. The men grew beards and demanded that the women wear the *hijab* and burkas. True, when the Indians came (often from East Africa, expelled by Idi Amin) they had a better education and a little money—not millions, as some Pakistanis

THE LAST DAYS OF EUROPE

claimed, but enough to open a lowly corner shop. But the Indians had drive and worked themselves up.

What could the authorities do to improve the chances of the Pakistanis? This question concerned not just Bradford but communities all over Britain and Western Europe. The authorities could not solve an identity crisis, but they could provide loans or grants to men and women submitting projects that seemed feasible for earning a livelihood. Even if only some of these projects succeeded, it would be a helpful investment. Above all, they could attempt by every means to make young members of this community attend school, to graduate and to continue education or training. They should be given special conditions in school because of their disadvantaged social background.

The British government has been running a "sure start" program in recent years, which, like the American Head Start, is an early childhood learning program that has been expanded and should be expanded even more. The same goes for English-language teaching and job advice centers. The administration of Prime Minister Tony Blair has strongly supported faith (Islamic) schools, even though a majority of the British oppose this. These schools are required to teach the national curriculum in addition to offering religious instruction. But there is no real control as to what is taught in these schools and whether their level is up to minimum standards. Another educational program (Aim Higher) concentrates on talented young people in deprived areas, trying to steer them toward good schools and universities. Muslim leaders have complained that so far those of African and Caribbean descent have mainly benefited from these schemes.

Perhaps financial rewards should be given not only to those who distinguish themselves at school but also to those who show any effort at all. Cynics may argue that more money can be made by drug peddling and larceny, but this, too, is a limited field, and if the authorities manage to reduce the number of social misfits in the streets and to give them the chance of a real job, this will be a major achievement. It certainly will not be fair compared to non-Muslims, but if one has to choose between justice and social peace, expediency will prevail. As Lee Jasper, the race adviser of London's mayor Ken Livingstone, said, "You have to treat people differently to treat them equally."

The British government, through the Home Office and other departments, has established various commissions and subcommittees recommending (and partly carrying out) a variety of measures ranging from citizenship lessons in Muslim schools and recruiting more Muslim police officers to offering family tax credits and affirmative action in employment and higher education, giving preference to those of a Muslim background. But in the last resort the initiative for positive change must come from within the Muslim community; state and local authorities can only facilitate this process. If parents do not support the education of their children—or, as in the case of their daughters, if parents frequently discourage or prohibit it—there is little the authorities can do. There have been no indications that an alternative Muslim leadership is likely to emerge any time soon.

The liberal and secular elements of Muslim society are weak, and the emerging Muslim middle class has not shown much interest in helping their compatriots or coreligionists who have been less fortunate. Many have distanced themselves physically from the community. The initiative of the British authorities to help gifted youngsters from the ghettos make their way to Oxford, Cambridge, and other top universities is most welcome. The idea behind this is, of course, that eventually these gifted young men and women will be teachers and youth leaders acting as role models. But how many of them will follow this road? The majority will probably find their way to greener pastures.

There are some secular Muslim intellectuals in Britain and some of them publish a glossy journal *(Q),* but the street is dominated by the followers of conservative and radical Islamist imams. Those praised by British politicians like Livingstone as models of an enlightened Islam, like the telepreacher Qaradawi, are reactionaries for whom even Tariq Ramadan is a near apostate. In brief, the fight for accommodation with the Muslim community in Britain is an uphill struggle. Many of the measures suggested to facilitate this could be helpful. Even the dialogue with the wrong leaders is perhaps not altogether useless, provided there are no illusions as to the basically illiberal character of these leaders and the narrow limits of their power and influence within their own communities.

The Future of Muslim Europe: France

IF MUSLIMS IN Britain are a relatively small minority, the situation in France is very different. The Muslim population of France is about 4 to 5 million. French authorities have been far stricter than the British in enforcing the (republican) law of the land. They deported imams who engaged in political incitement (some were back after a short while). They made no concession with regard to wearing the *hijab* in school or introducing single-sex schools. Their policy has been one of integration and assimilation rather than multiculturalism. This has resulted on one hand in far more widespread conflicts and physical clashes than in Britain. On the other

hand, it has also resulted in the emergence of a much more substantial secular sector of Muslim origins.

Not much is heard of them because they are not among the
rioters nor are they likely to be interviewed by the media. But the
rate of mixed marriages is higher in France than in Britain and terrorism inside France has been less than in Britain. More second-,
third-, and fourth-generation Muslim immigrants have become as-
similated, entered the civil service or local administration, and
made their way in French social and cultural life. Whole groups
such as the Kabyles (Berbers) from North Africa have not been part
of the Muslim revolt of the *banlieues*. But this also meant that they
have often moved out and distanced themselves from the Muslim
community.

There are more no-go zones in France than in Britain, and
political scientists believe that France faces balkanization in the not
too distant future. It is probably more difficult to predict the future
of France than of any other European country because of the urgent need of reform—and the great resistance to it. It is equally
difficult to envisage real balkanization—that is to say, the emergence of separate states or autonomous regions on the soil of
France. Islamist radicals may want full power in regions in which
Muslims constitute a majority, but these are poor areas, with mass
unemployment, and who would pay for their upkeep?

For this reason, even Muslim radicals may be compelled to
oppose further immigration to France, for the more needy there
are, the less the state will be able to help. Perhaps the development
will be in the direction of binational autonomous regions. The
Muslims may make concessions with regard to the sharia, and the
French authorities may give up the old republican model with a
clear division between church and state. There have been cities and
regions in France in which ethnic coexistence has somehow

worked, such as, for instance, Marseille, a model that ought to be studied.

All kind of political coalitions could be envisaged. The communists and the New Left have tried hard to gain supporters among the Muslim community, but they have not been very successful. A poll carried out by Skyrock, a radio station popular in the "zone," led to a strange result. When listeners were asked for whom they would vote, Jean-Marie Le Pen, leader of the nationalist National Front, was the first choice, Donadieu, a famous anti-Jewish clown who is half French, half Senegalese, came in second, and Interior Minister Nicolas Sarkozy placed third. No other politician was in the running. Perhaps one or more Muslim political parties will emerge, but if this should come to pass, the divisions in the Muslim community that were not very visible in the past will come out in the open—differences, for instance, between those from black and North Africa, even between those of Algerian and Moroccan origin. It seems more likely that the existing political parties will compete for the Muslim vote.

At present there are no strong political organizations among the Muslim communities, and in their absence "direct" rather than political action seems most likely. Following the riots of 2005, all kind of advice has been offered to the French government by international organizations such as the International Crisis Group (ICG). These suggestions include "revising public housing allocation by promoting ethnic intermixing." But it is doubtful whether those concerned will embrace ethnic intermixing with great enthusiasm. Nor is it clear how "the harsh cuts that have affected the public financing of associations since 2002" can be revised and reduced in a period of economic crisis and financial retrenchment without hurting the needy of other groups. Such a policy would aggravate rather than relieve ethnic tensions. Interior Minister

Nicolas Sarkozy, the most outspoken French politician and the bête noire of Islamist activists, has promoted a policy of positive discrimination, meaning giving preferential treatment to Muslims. This was opposed by most of the French establishment. But it may become official policy in the years to come. Whether this will be enough to maintain social and political peace is uncertain. On many occasions the French Socialists have expressed goodwill and compassion for the Muslim immigrants, but their policy is not significantly different from that of other French parties.

It is difficult to blame them, for there are no obvious solutions.

The Future of Muslim Europe: Germany

THE SITUATION OF Muslim immigrant communities in Germany is more hopeful in some respects, more depressing in others. To take Berlin, which has the biggest Turkish community (Kreuzberg, Neukölln, Wedding), those who made it socially and economically are more inclined to stay in their quarters and to invest in them. There are Turkish banks and travel agencies, shops, and medical practices. They are less likely to become slums than the British inner-city districts or the French suburbs ("the zone"). But it should also be noted that in cities such as Duisburg the state of affairs is less encouraging.

In the beginning there were few Turkish enterprises other than little wooden kiosks selling *döner,* vegetables, and fruit, but gradually small and medium-size businesses appeared. Some sixty thousand enterprises developed, most of them very small family businesses. But there are also some megabusinesses, and names like that of Kemal Sahin, who studied engineering and became head of a big holding company, are well-known outside their community. Turkish immigrants of the second and third generation have entered politics, are authors of widely read books, have received awards for the best movie of the year, and so on. The number of "mixed marriages" has doubled, to about 8,000, compared with 4,000 before the year 2000.

But with all this, the integration of Turkish immigrants has been anything but a success story; cultural alienation is probably worse than in Britain and France in the absence of a common language (most immigrants to the United Kingdom know some English, and virtually all immigrants to France know some French). The unemployment rate among young people of Turkish origin is more than twice that of others. Eighty-five percent of Turkish and Arab residents belong to the underclass. The educational situation is particularly discouraging. In 1985, some 86 percent of young Turks under the age of twenty-one went to school; today that rate is only about 40 percent. The number of those who do not finish any school, even the *Hauptschule*—the refuge of those who have failed—is high and rising. Their knowledge of German is deficient; their social framework is the street gang.

The rate of juvenile crime is two to three times higher than that of other sectors of the population. True, some 24,000 Turks study in German universities—that number constitutes 8 percent of this age cohort (18 to 25). This is still quite small in comparison with the percentage of young Germans of that age, but it is one of the rays of hope in an otherwise bleak picture. The situation in places outside Berlin is worse—in cities such as Duisburg (whose Turkish section is Marxlohe), Hamburg (Wilhelmsburg), or even Cologne (Kalk and Ehrenfeld).

After more than four decades the situation in the Turkish communities in Germany is worse than in many Turkish cities—for instance, concerning the status of women. The influence of the most reactionary political and religious groups is stronger among the Turkish communities in Germany than in Turkey proper, while the impact of the progressive secular forces is weaker. Whereas in Turkey the army command, the judiciary, and most of the intelligentsia serve as a counterforce to the Islamists, there are no such forces among the Turks in Germany. Turkish intellectuals in Germany do not have much influence in their own communities; their books are read by Germans rather than their compatriots and offer no serious competition to the sermons of the imams. The few courageous Turkish women who fight for at least partial emancipation of their female compatriots are considered traitors, physically threatened, and virtually excluded from the community.

What can be done, what should be done, to improve the situation? The German government through the citizenship law of 2000 has made it far easier for Turks to acquire German citizenship. Some 160,000 have availed themselves annually of this right. Candidates for citizenship have to undergo certain examinations concerning minimal language proficiency and knowledge of the basic laws.

These examinations have been criticized by some and, on the one hand, it is indeed true that a person can be a good citizen even if he or she does not know the name of Germany's main rivers or is not familiar with the leading figures in German literature. On the other hand, unless the individual has a certain minimal knowledge of the language, he or she will (unless there are special circumstances) have great difficulties in obeying the law and enjoying his or her rights as a citizen. It is useful to know, furthermore, that Germany is located in Europe, that it is a democracy, and that the sharia is not the law of the land. Virtually every country in the world has such tests, including the United States. (The present writer, a professor of history, failed to give the correct answer in two instances concerning amendments to the U.S. Constitution.) In Britain it was the rule that a police inspector would visit the homes of candidates for naturalization to find out, among other things, whether the children in the household went to school and had a working knowledge of English.

German society (like the British and French) has been made responsible for the failure of integration and the existence of the ghettos. It is certainly true that few Germans received the new immigrants with open arms; after all, the Germans were never asked in the first place and in later years found it difficult to accept that the presence of millions of "foreigners" was not a temporary phenomenon, but they were there to stay. The German government is spending at the present time some 100 million euros annually to promote integration, which, for all one knows, is not remotely enough to help solve what is becoming the most pressing domestic problem.

But it is not at all clear whether the result would have been radically different even if a sum ten times as large had been invested. For a considerable majority of Turkish immigrants emphatically did not want their children to live like Germans and it stands to reason that to achieve this aim the self-imposed ghetto was the best framework to protect the fold from temptation. Most Turkish parents, having little education themselves, showed little interest in the education of their children.

Only few joined parent-teacher associations to help with life in school. The children of other immigrant groups faced initial difficulties in mastering the language, but in many cases with the help of teachers the parents organized extra after-school study sessions so that their children could quickly catch up. Only few such initiatives have been reported from among the Turkish communities. When asked about their lack of response and cooperation, one could hear all too frequently that in order to live in the ghetto a knowledge of German was no vital necessity. There are three local Turkish-language television channels in addition to those that can be watched from Turkey, not to mention Turkish-language newspapers printed locally. When conscientious teachers in Berlin insisted on the use of German both during and between classes, they were accused by zealous German multiculturalists of practicing cultural repression and depriving these children of their cultural heritage, and worse. (Many of these pupils went to religious school after classes in the state schools.)

The misfortune of Germany was not that it received millions of immigrants but that these came from the most backward, least educated sectors of Turkish society. What prevents a more or less successful absorption of these immigrants is the combination of social factors and the dead hand of fundamentalist religion, which wants to preserve its influence and which can do so only by shutting itself off from alien influences. For many Turkish immigrants of the older generation the mosque is still not just the religious center of their life but also the cultural, social, and political center. However, many mosques have been under the influence of Islamist-nationalist groups such as Milli Goerues, and some thirty throughout Germany have been under constant observation for suspicion of preaching jihadism. (Up to 2001, mosques, like churches, enjoyed a special status in this respect and could not be observed by state security organs, but this changed following terrorist attacks in Europe, Asia, and America.) It is clear that the key to success is education. Education and the acquisition of skills do not automatically make for loyalty with their adopted country but greatly improve the chances for social and economic betterment and thus at least a potential beginning of integration. Unless the hold of fundamentalist groups and their political indoctrination is broken—and it is doubtful whether the German authorities have the political will to do so—there will be no progress.

Social workers and planners have submitted over the years hundreds and thousands of proposals for the improvement of the situation of the immigrants. They have suggested confidence-building measures through "intercultural meetings" to gain the support of those living in predominantly (or exclusively) immigrant quarters, the removal of the stigma attached at present to the ghettos, and improvement of the infrastructure in these quarters. Some believe that the existence of the ghettos does not necessarily impede an improvement of the situation, while others think that these concentrations constitute a serious obstacle. Never before in the history of migration has there been so much concern and planning. But the results have been meager, much of the debate has been on an abstract level, and there has been little open speaking. The only issue on which there seems to be full agreement is that some problems will be easier to solve if the economy improves, which, unfortunately, cannot be taken for granted.

Spain

DIFFERENT EUROPEAN COUNTRIES have been dealing with their Muslim minorities in different ways, often through benign neglect, as in the case of Spain and Italy. The number of Muslims (mostly North African) living in Spain is not known, but it is probably close to 1 million. They are concentrated in the south of Spain and the major cities. The Zapatero Socialist government in Spain has legalized the status of the illegal immigrants in Spain, some 700,000 of them, in the hope that this would contribute to normalization. But the pressure of migrants continued in 2005–6: Many tried to enter the Spanish Ceuta and Melilla enclaves in North Africa, storming walls, and others attempted to reach the Canary Islands from Africa. Spanish negotiations with Morocco, where most of the Muslim migrants originated, have been only partly successful. Many thousands of illegal immigrants from sub-Saharan Africa made their way to the Canary Islands, which served as an entry gate to Spain and to Europe; negotiations with African governments were equally fruitless.

Unemployment in Morocco is high, and there has been constant pressure to enter Europe on the part of not only unskilled workers but also young people with higher education. While there have been few complaints on the part of Muslims in Spain about police molestation and "Islamophobia" (despite the traditional negative attitude toward the Moros), there has been little social integration. The Spanish government has established a foundation to help minority religions to integrate in Spanish society, mainly by means of language courses. But its initial budget was a symbolic $3.5 million—compared with more than a billion dollars that the French government allocated for special education. The Spanish authorities have not opposed wearing the *hijab* in school and have accepted Muslim religious teachings in school but have not been paying for Muslim teachers of religion. This, like the funds for the mosques, is apparently covered through major contributions from Saudi Arabia and Libya. Most of the mosques preach a mainstream version of Islam, but there have been reports about others engaging in radical indoctrination.

There are many indications that terrorist sleeper cells exist in Spain, but with the exception of the Madrid attacks in March 2004 there have been no major terrorist attacks, nor, with one or two exceptions, have there been anti-Muslim activities.

The Spanish, like the French Muslim communities, are relatively homogeneous; the majority come from North Africa, with a sprinkling from sub-Saharan Africa. However, the country of origin also continues to play a certain role—Moroccans (the majority) put the emphasis on their origin from this country, and Algerians no less so. In the case of Algeria there are significant differences with the Berber-Kabyle population, who think of themselves not as a tribe but as a separate people. In the Muslim organizations there has been frequent conflict on these lines. In other European countries the communities are far more heterogeneous, and while non-Muslims tend to pay little attention to these differences, they often play an important role in inter-Muslim affairs.

Ethnic divisions inside European Muslim communities are considerable but tend to be overlooked. More than a third of the Muslims living in Austria came from Bosnia and Kosovo. Muslims in Belgium are partly of Turkish, partly of Moroccan origin, with other countries of origin also represented. The situation in the Netherlands is similar. Among Muslims living in Italy, more than a quarter are Albanians. While there is some mixing between these various groups, they often stick together in their own housing estates, self-help, and social and sports organizations. There have been tensions on both the collective and the individual level, for instance, between Turks and Kurds in Germany, often generated by conflict in their home country. In brief, while the outside world tends to think of the Muslim communities as more or less monolithic, they are in fact constituted of a variety of disparate elements that have certain common interests but also experience tension and conflict.

Dreaming of a United Europe

AFTER THE NEW European constitution had been voted down in France and the Netherlands in 2005 it was decided to have a lengthy pause for reflection—there was little else that could have been done. Some, like France's interior minister, Nicolas Sarkozy, were saying that a new initiative toward closer cooperation must come from a new activist core consisting of Germany and France and perhaps also Spain and Italy. (But France had just voted down the EU constitution.) It was clear to almost everyone that the original federal idea of the "United States of Europe," which, one way or another, had been the aim of the founding fathers after World War II, was no longer feasible when the European Union consisted of twenty-seven members.

Some suggested a new Plan D, but it was also clear that the real problem was not finding new wording that would placate those who feared a loss of sovereignty or even national or cultural identity. The real problem was that a new push could come only on the basis of a new psychological orientation, a new mood, a new attitude toward Europe. Basically everyone was in favor of some kind of unified Europe, but there was no agreement where its borders should be. Above all, whenever the interests of the nation-state and Europe collided, the interests of the former always came first. This emerged on every occasion, and just one recent illustration should suffice.

In early 2006 a meeting took place to deal with the establishment of a common European energy market. Everyone agreed on the need for a common policy. Even at present, Europe depends on imports from abroad for half of its energy. In the next twenty years, the North Sea oil and gas reserves will be exhausted, at which point dependence will increase to 70 percent or more. The dependence on natural gas imports from Russian and Algeria (and on oil imports from the Persian Gulf countries) is a matter of not only economic but also political importance. One of the heads of government (Lech Kaczynski of Poland) proposed the establishment of an energy NATO to provide some mutual help in an emergency, but this idea had no more chance for success than all the other proposals. The EU members were simply not ready to leave to Brussels the right to decide on issues like nuclear energy and, indeed, all others. The governments saw their main task as protecting their national oil and gas companies from takeover by other European firms; it was as if the Common Market no longer existed.

And if there was not a minimum of willingness to cooperate in the field of energy, there was even less of a cooperative spirit regarding foreign and defense policy. The political weakness of Europe had appeared starkly at the time of the Balkan wars. Soft power had been tried, but the diplomatic attempts to stop the fighting led nowhere. There was no European intervention capacity, and later on European countries had to act within a NATO framework under U.S. leadership. There simply was no alternative.

This realization of weakness led to a decision on the Common Foreign and Security Policy (CFSP) and even the appointment of a High Representative who should eventually become the European foreign minister. But no such minister has been appointed so far, and it is not likely that there will be such a person in the near future. And even if there should be such an appointment, what could the poor man or woman do? Is it at all likely that twenty-seven countries will agree on common political or military action? And even if they were to agree, they still would not have a credible intervention capacity. Europe will remain dependent for its energy supplies on Russia and the Middle East and will be threatened by new nuclear powers.

In brief, there are no realistic prospects for any significant advance in this direction. A Belgian prime minister (Guy Verhofstadt) has said that if Europe truly wants to be a world player, it must become even more closely integrated. Whether Europe truly wants this is not certain. From time to time voices to this effect are heard, especially at times of crisis, but by and large there seems to be no overwhelming support for the idea. Even if such support existed, Europe is not willing to pay the price for becoming a world player. But why make such an effort? There is, after all, no common foreign and security policy in Latin America, either, and the continent has not suffered any major ill effects. Perhaps the storms of the years to come will bypass Europe (as they bypassed Latin America); perhaps there will not be any storms at all. But what if there should be another Middle Eastern war? What would Europe do other than wring its hands in the event of such a calamity? The farcical and wholly ineffectual negotiations between the European Union and Tehran about the Iranian nuclear buildup may well be an indication of the shape of things to come.

It goes without saying that this policy is shortsighted, but is there any chance for an early change in European resolve? A major crisis could trigger a new dynamism and there are, unfortunately, a great number of major potential crises—economic, political, and military—that might occur. But they could also lead to defeatism, to the claim that Europe is too weak for decisive action and that it can no longer play a leading role in world politics—in brief, they could lead to abdication.

The more time passes, the more difficult achieving a common foreign and defense policy may become. For chances are that, given current demographic trends, European states are moving in different directions. The ethnic composition of the population of France or Netherlands twenty years from now will be different, and this could have a substantial impact on its domestic and foreign policy and even on its relations with their neighbors. It could also lead to a new exodus of Jews from Europe. But there are not that many left, and by taking a low profile they might be able to survive in the new conditions.

Salvaging the Welfare State

OPINIONS OF LEADING economists concerning the future of the welfare state (social Europe, the social model) range from bleak pessimism (the welfare state is dead and cannot be resuscitated) to relative optimism: By a mixture of modest cuts of benefits and modest tax increases, the essentials of the welfare state can be saved. All European countries had to cut benefits for two decades; this was started by conservative governments (Margaret Thatcher's in Britain, Helmut Kohl's in Germany, Carl Bildt's in Sweden) but the social democratic governments that followed them had to follow the same policies. The services provided became permanently more expensive. This was, on the one hand, the result of more people living longer and the higher costs of medical services. On the other hand, it was also the result of slow growth or stagnation. When the welfare state was first conceived, expenditures were considerably less and growth was more substantial.

Government cuts provoked bitter resentment in all countries

and active opposition; a political party like the German Social Democrats under Gerhard Schroeder that tried to adopt reforms (i.e., cuts) was bound to be defeated in the next elections. But their opponents would not be more successful; they could give in to a public outcry by going deeper into debt, but this was untenable in the longer run and also contrary to the rules of the European Union. Or they could increase taxes, but taxes in most European countries were already high (close to 50 percent) and further increases would slow down economic growth and cause more unemployment. The policy suggested by the far left—soak the rich—was not practical, either. True, at a time of economic crisis, growing disparities in income were difficult to justify; why should members of Parliament receive pensions that were five or six times higher than the average? But there were not enough rich people to be soaked so that it would make a decisive difference overall. And if companies or individuals were squeezed too hard, there was the danger (nay, the probability) that they would relocate to countries with lower taxation.

In brief, there seemed to be no easy solution to the dilemma; in fact, there seemed to be no solution at all—without a dramatic improvement in the economic situation of the country. The only alternative was a political-social covenant between all those concerned to show moderation and to accept the necessity, however painful, of cuts in order to preserve at least some of the essentials of the welfare state. Such agreement seems easier in some countries than in others—in Sweden and to a certain extent in the Netherlands such a compact worked despite much grumbling. In Germany and especially in France there is enormous resistance to giving up any of the achievements of the welfare state. Populists put the blame on globalization and the vagaries of the market economy. But they have no answers to the problems facing

Europe—a command economy and economic nationalism are unlikely to solve the problems.

Aside from the general European situation, there is a generational problem for which no answer has been found. As more people live longer and as the labor force is shrinking, the burden of taking care of the expenditures for the elderly rests more heavily on the young, and this burden, too, is likely to grow. An intergenerational compact will be needed not only in Europe but in all developed countries.

Toward Binational States?

A VARIETY OF solutions over time can be envisaged for making progress on the road to European unity. The same is true, despite all the difficulties, with regard to remodeling the welfare state, reducing it in scope but making it affordable. The demographic changes that will take place, however, seem irreversible. The question that arises is not whether they will take place but what impact they will have on Europe's future. Auguste Comte, the father of modern sociology, is often quoted to the effect that demography is fate, and Spengler's famous *Decline of the West* ends with a quotation from Seneca: *Ducunt fata volentem, nolentem trahunt volentem ducunt* ("Fate leads the willing, and drags the unwilling"). True, Fate sometimes changes direction, but he who has eyes to see must be aware by now that the face of Europe is changing, and not only in the major cities: The Muslim enclaves in Berlin and Milan, in Madrid and Stockholm, and in London and Copenhagen are spreading. As the Dutch minister of justice has said, if a majority of Dutchmen opt for the sharia at some future date, this has to be respected.

To inspect the Muslim heartland where a majority can be expected before midcentury, one ought to take a walk in one of the cities of the Ruhr and then leave by way of the Autobahn either straight west in the direction of Eindhoven and beyond or, alternatively, in a northwesterly direction toward Nijmegen and Utrecht and the English Channel. Starting at Dortmund and Duisburg, one passes northern France and southern Belgium, the major Dutch cities (Amsterdam, Rotterdam, Utrecht), and the old heavy-industry and textile centers such as the conurbation of Lille/Roubaix/Tourcoing with more than 1.5 million residents. In addition there are major enclaves in Britain such as Bradford/Burnley/Oldham or at Malmö in Sweden and also a number of cities in southern Spain and southern France. Some of these regions are gradually coming to resemble the less savory parts of North Africa and the Middle East. I doubt whether Georges Simenon, who was born in Liège about a hundred years ago, would recognize the scenes of his childhood.

Such demographic changes are by no means unique. In the United States, New York no longer has a "white" majority, nor does Los Angeles, and in a few decades Greater Washington and San Francisco could also be in this category. But there is an important difference inasmuch as the United States is a country of immigrants, accustomed to coexistence of various ethnic groups. New York, Washington, Chicago, and Los Angeles have had black mayors. Furthermore, in the United States it will not be a question of one specific ethnic group gaining supremacy. If the "white" will lose predominance, so will the black, for the ethnic groups gaining are Latinos and Asians. Furthermore, while America may no longer be a melting-pot intermingling of ethnic groups, no group seeks to impose its religion or religious law or way of life on others. There are social tensions, but calls for jihad would not find a great response. The business of ethnic America is to make a comfortable living, not to fight—except perhaps turf fights among gangs and the criminal underworld. There are ghettos in America, but there is also a black and Latino middle class moving out of them. As for the emigrants from the Far East, they have been doing better than almost any other group in business, the professions, and education. Emigrants from Muslim countries, mostly educated and middle-class, have also been doing much better in the United States than in Europe.

How will the transition in Europe take place? Is the trend toward disintegration? It would be an exaggeration to argue that immigrants from Pakistan and Turkey, from the Arab East and North Africa, have been a uniform failure, socially and economical-ly. While there are only a few statistics, it is known that there are 5,400 millionaires among Muslims in Britain (their total assets are believed to be about 6 billion pounds sterling). Among the list of Russian billionaires we find not only Mikhail Fridman and Roman Abramovich but also Alisher Usmanov (2.6 billion), Suleiman Keri-mov (7.1), and Iskander Mahmudov (4.5). There are wealthy Turks in Germany and wealthy North Africans in France.

There is a small middle class of Muslim origin developing wherever Muslim communities exist. But it is also true that for the time being the ghetto prevails; so, too, do unemployment among the young generation and dependence on handouts from state and municipality. The religious leadership is trying very hard to keep their flock together, and this can be achieved only if the ghetto per-sists, if there is little, if any, contact between the faithful and the infidels. The young are indoctrinated from an early age, and many of those in Germany, the Netherlands, and Scandinavia know no more of the language of the land than necessary for daily use. (But their knowledge of the native language of their parents is also usu-ally rather weak.)

What follows from this unfortunate state of affairs? It is generally believed that in view of their declining birthrate, most countries of Europe will need immigrants in the years to come. But it seems pointless to look for immigrants without skills and education, which would only swell the army of the unemployed and unemployable; European societies will not be in a position to support them. What is needed are immigrants showing both ability and ambition, and attempts should be made to attract those likely to make a positive contribution to Western societies as well as to their own betterment.

Educators in Europe who have closely followed the education of young Muslims believe that the older ones among them (the young men in particular) are largely a lost generation. The emphasis should be on the education of the younger ones, with regard to acquiring both language skills and a general education. True, the younger generation has developed a subculture of their own that is expressed, for instance, in their songs and language, sometimes imitated by their white contemporaries, who think it cool. But the rapping, misogynistic and homophobic, is as ugly as their language, consisting mainly of expletives and curses, the lingo of the underworld, wholly devoid of even a trace of humor, as in Cockney or the Berlin patois.

While a deep knowledge of German, French, or British culture cannot be expected from most candidates for citizenship—how many of the natives would fail such examinations?—it stands to reason that a working knowledge of the language as well as of the laws and way of life should be a precondition. It could well be that in another generation or two, when the former minorities will outnumber native Germans or Dutch or French in certain parts of these countries, the discussions about integration will no longer make sense; having become a minority, the "natives" cannot expect the majority to adjust themselves to their way of life, to their language and laws. It will be up to the "natives" to become integrated into a changed society. This stage has not been reached yet, but it is certainly not too early to ponder the character of the new society and the implications likely to emerge.

In the regions in which Muslims will be a majority, there will be a demand for autonomy. Separatism, the demand for full independence, is unlikely, even if only due to the depressed economic situation in these regions. They will be the new authorities on the local and regional level, but they will expect the state to accept responsibility for the social well-being of the inhabitants; without this there will be at best impoverishment, at worst a breakdown. Perhaps in due time these Muslim societies will produce an elite of entrepreneurs, of scientists and technologists second to none, the Einsteins and the Nobel Prize winners of tomorrow, providing a major economic and cultural impetus to these societies. But at present it is difficult to point even to the beginnings of such a trend.

Even if the demand to introduce Muslim religious law (the sharia) as the new law of the land is pressed, exemptions will be granted to the non-Muslims. True, there have been demands for radical Islamization in some circles (for instance in the United Kingdom), but there is no unanimity on these lines even within the Muslim community. In other words, the emergence of binational states seems more likely even if they have not worked well at all elsewhere.

The Muslim communities are, to repeat once again, divided along religious and national lines. Even in Germany within the Turkish community there is the division between Turkish Sunnis on one hand and significant minorities such as the Kurds (at least half a million) and the Alawites on the other hand. There are important differences between the religion practiced by Moroccans and Turks in the Netherlands and Belgium, between Pakistanis in Britain and Muslims from the Middle East in Britain, even between those of Algerian origin in France and those from Morocco. This list could be extended, and there have been complaints that political and religious leaders from one country (or one sect—for instance, Turks in Belgium and Arabs in Britain) have acquired influence out of proportion to the size of the ethnic group to which they belong. It will be up to the Muslim communities to find a common denominator; there will be a struggle for influence and power, and the outcome is not at all certain.

"Eurabia" (for an Arab Muslim Europe) is an interesting term but largely misleading, for it does not apply to Germany, nor to Britain, nor to several other European countries. For Turks are not Arabs, and their attitude toward Arabs is anything but friendly. The gang warfare in the streets of Turkish Berlin between groups of Turkish, Arab, and Kurdish adolescents does not reflect any particular closeness between these communities. Nor are Pakistanis that well disposed toward Arabs, even though politicians and preachers of Arab origin have imposed themselves with some success on Muslim communities in the United Kingdom and other countries. Arab ambitions to dominate Muslim communities in Europe have generated opposition. In the United Kingdom, national identity is no longer an educational aim, and neither is integration; given the ethnic constitution of the immigrant population, the South Asian element will be a stronger force in shaping the face and the character of the future Britain than will the Arab.

Nor is it certain how strong the impetus toward religious fundamentalism and radicalism will be in the years to come. There is reason to assume that it will lose momentum. The radicalism of the young generation may manifest itself in religious terms, but it is doubtful whether it is religious in inspiration. Complaints to this effect have come from religious leaders inside the Muslim community all over Europe. They have argued that the knowledge of things Islamic among the young generation is limited and so is the urge to know more about it. It concerns above all the young generation, but also those who for one reason or another have left the ghetto, either because they managed to climb up the social ladder or for other reasons.

As Muslims face the temptations of Western societies, this process of cultural and political assimilation is inevitable; the question is how quickly it will proceed. Among the intellectuals there is the growing distaste for a religion that has, under the impact of radical interpreters, become more primitive and identified above all with political violence directed against innocent civilians. Among women, however orthodox, there is increasing demand for an Islam that gives them more rights than the fundamentalists are willing to grant.

As for the young men, a leading Berlin imam said that the road to the mosque is long and the temptations many. This refers to drugs, crime, sex, and other seductions of the decadent West. Decadence is attractive and infectious. In Britain and in France young Muslims are now substantially involved not only in the trade of drugs but also as consumers. The same young Muslim who threatens his sister with a beating (or worse) unless she dresses modestly with a *hijab* will by no means necessarily disdain Western pornography. According to Saudi authorities, of the 2.2 million Internet users in the Kingdom, some 92 percent wish to access forbidden or indecent material, which almost always refers not to atheist Web sites but to pornography (*Arab News,* October 2, 2005). Such figures may not be unnaturally high in comparison with other countries, as the Saudi authorities have pointed out. But these figures certainly point to the deeply ambivalent attitude toward the forbidden on the part of the young Muslim male, the attraction becoming even stronger because of the seductive attraction of what is forbidden. ("They close doors and we get in through the windows" is a frequent comment.) There is furthermore in Arab medieval literature something like a *Kama Sutra* tradition (Omar Ibn Abi Rabi'a, Ibn Hazm Andalou, and, later on, Ibn Foulayta), which will no doubt be rediscovered one of these days.

The Beatles played a modest part in the downfall of the Soviet empire; in a similar way Arab pop (such as Fun^Da^Mental, Natasha Atlas, Akhnaton, IAM) is perhaps helping to undermine Muslim fundamentalism. In the 1980s musical entertainment (including any kind of compact disc) was strictly banned by the Muslim Brotherhood in Egypt and elsewhere, and as late as 2003 the performances of Nancy Ajram, probably the best known belly dancer in the Arab world, were banned by the Egyptian parliament on all state television channels. But she and her colleagues can still be seen in hundreds of thousands, if not millions, of video clips and on countless private satellite TV channels such as Rotana TV, Nagham, or Melody Hits, broadcasting twenty-four hours a day and reaching a very wide audience. An Arab pop scene has emerged in the Middle East and among the Muslim communities in Europe in defiance of all the bans and fatwas. True, the lyrics of the European Muslim rappers contain lines from the Koran and nationalist slogans ("I am a soldier in the army of Allah"—or of Malcolm X or of Louis Farrakhan), but they also rap lines of sexism, antiwhite racism, and praise of gang rape. A comparative study of these lyrics is instructive; whereas the Middle Eastern (in Arabic) are mainly entertainment, the European (above all the French) are far more politicized, full of hate and brutality.

What makes the subculture of gangsta rap and hip-hop suspect to Muslim fundamentalists is the non-Muslim (Afro-Caribbean) inspiration of this music and perhaps also the fact that some of the leading figures of this scene are not Muslim by origin but Italian (Akhnaton), Copt (Mutamassik), or even Jewish (Natasha Atlas). As for the artistic sophistication of this subculture, the Beirut professor may well be right who argued that the worst aspects of Western mass culture have been copied, not the best. Fundamentalist leaders found it easy to ostracize Western ideologies from liberalism to Marxism, but they have been powerless vis-à-vis the pop scene and soccer.

There is nothing in the Koran about street gangs, but this phenomenon (as well as gang warfare) in the Muslim street in Europe is quite important and has been insufficiently studied so far. These gangs have appeared in many parts of the world, and various factors have been adduced to explain this phenomenon—dysfunctional families, personal traits, human instincts, child abuse, urbanization, identity politics, and exposure to violence in the culture in which they grew up. Ethnic factors play a role, too, and some cultures are more prone to violence than others. There has been generational conflict in many societies, but whereas in Germany, for instance, it was directed against the tyrannical father and teacher (as in the youth movement of the 1900s), among the Islamic minority it is now directed against "the other." In the European Muslim communities, gangs may have economic motives (e.g., drug trafficking) as well as psychological ones (satisfaction through display of machismo, protection of the turf).

These gangs are far more often found in the second and third generation of immigrants, and this is connected with the retreat of the state, which in democratic societies no longer has a monopoly on violence. In authoritarian regimes, short shrift is made of troublemakers, irrespective of age and gender. In contemporary demo-

cratic societies they do not have much to fear: In Western European societies the police are under strict restraints, as are teachers at
school and judges at court. The perpetrators are bound to be re-
leased within days, if not hours, and their very arrest turns them
into heroes among their comrades; young Muslim gang members
when interviewed have talked with contempt of their "white" contemporaries who will seldom resist when attacked and robbed.
These Muslim gang members' aggressiveness is bound to give
them the respect they are craving.

The gang phenomenon has had an important political
dimension—for instance, among Latinos in South and North
America and the South African gangs in Soweto and elsewhere—
and the same is true today. But as far as gang ideology is concerned, how much of it is Islamism and how much hip-hop culture
and gangsta rap? It has widely been reported from various countries that the young enforcers of the sharia have also been dealing
drugs and consuming them, engaging in sex practices not at all legitimate according to their religion, and listening constantly to rap
music, which is also in contravention to strict Islam. The language
of rap certainly is not the language of religion, nor of sacred spirituality, which Prince Charles recently invoked (see below), but of
the criminal underworld. True, some Islamists have gone out to the
gangs and prison inmates in an attempt to convert them, but the
gangs have also invaded the mosques to find new members. It is
not at all clear who will prevail in this competition. While all this
has been predominantly a young male preserve, girls have also par-
ticipated in some of these activities, particularly in school; this, too,
apparently has to do with the urge to gain respect or at least not to
be considered "whores" *(Schlampen, putains)* by the young males
had they stood aside during an attack.

There have been many mutterings on the part of young

British and French Muslims about the formalistic and joyless character of their religion, the endless, parrotlike repetition of prayers. As one young British Muslim said in an interview, expressing what probably many of his contemporaries thought, their religion demands too much of them. They would like to do what their secular friends do, to have boyfriends and girlfriends, to go occasionally to the cinema, to watch television, to play video games, not to live in social and cultural isolation.

But they are unlikely to enter disputations about the hermeneutics of the Koran with the imams. Far more likely, young Muslims will gradually drop out or limit their religion to lip service out of respect for their parents and families. The next cultural war will not be between believers and infidels but within the camp of the believers, as religious belief erodes not so much through open defiance but by stealth. This erosion of religious orthodoxy and fanaticism will certainly not affect all, however; there will be fanatics who, for all one knows, may redouble their militancy.

As Muslim communities are growing in numbers and will spread, how are non-Muslims likely to react? Some will move out—this is a process that began years ago—from London's East End, from sections of Dortmund and Cologne, from many parts of the Paris *banlieues*. Such internal migration apart, there has been emigration from the Netherlands and elsewhere to countries in which they are less likely to be exposed to a way of life they find unpleasant to accept; it is impossible to say to what extent this process will grow in the future.

Political coexistence will probably be easier to achieve than social coexistence. Most political parties will compete for Muslim votes, and some might be taken over by Muslims. There are certain common interests and there could be coalitions. In some places the Muslim vote could be decisive even now (as shown, for instance, by the victory of the socialist PVDA—the Dutch Labor Party—in Holland in 2006, where half of the counselors nominated and elected were of Muslim origin) and it will be even more important in the future. Would Ken Livingstone, the mayor of London, have been elected without the Muslim vote? Muslims have a quarter of the representation in the Brussels regional parliament, and one of them, a woman, was elected mayor. There is the danger of polarization; local elections in London's East End in 2006 showed an increase in the xenophobic vote, the British National Party on one hand and the Trotskyite-Islamist groups on the other.

Left-wing parties have tried particularly hard to gain a following in the Muslim communities, but while there is a strong populist element in radical Islam, these are marriages of convenience that may not last long. The anticapitalism and antiglobalism of radical Islam are rooted in a radical right-wing, reactionary ideology in which extreme conservative elements prevail.

An anti-Muslim backlash from the extreme right seems probable on a regional basis; Antwerp (Anvers) serves as an example, as do the Black Country in Britain and London's East End, as well as Barking and Dagenham (white working-class neighborhoods), parts of Birmingham, and the electoral successes of the Front National in France (Drieux, Orange, Vitrolles, and other cities). But it is doubtful whether this backlash will have decisive nationwide consequences. Works of political science fiction have presented scenarios in which Muslims (and Jews) have been expelled on twenty-four hours' notice from Belgium (Jacques Neirynck, *Le siège de Bruxelles,* Paris, 1996). In a similar vein, following the French riots in November 2005, a French "politthriller" (political thriller) appeared (Clément Weill-Rayna, *Le songe du guerrier,* Paris, 2006) about a right-wing backlash. Such a backlash seems likely, and not only in France, but that these extreme forces will come to power seems about as likely as Russian fantasies about France becoming a radical Islamic state with a small Christian minority resisting underground—to be eventually saved by Russian armed forces (Elena Chudinova, *Mechet Parizhskoi bogomateri* [The Mosque of Notre Dame de Paris], Moscow, 2005). Faithful Christians are confined to a ghetto, musical instruments and pictures are destroyed, nothing works anymore in Paris, and even the Metro has come to a standstill.

Political speculations frequently rest on the assumption that there will be a monolithic Muslim bloc, which, as has been stressed earlier, does not correspond with the facts. With all the religious-political radicalization of recent years, there are many centrifugal trends inside this community and internal competition and rivalry. In many ways it is a race against time. It is partly a question of the durability of fanaticism; these waves inspired by religions or secular religions do not last forever. The fanaticism of Muslim communities in Europe should not be overrated. There is sympathy for the so-called militants; there is frustration and aggression and the desire to manifest the discontent. But the majority of Muslims do not want to die a martyr's death but rather lead a quiet and reasonably comfortable life. How to promote the peaceful trends in the European Muslim communities? It is above all a question of raising the level of education of these communities, of inducing them to think for themselves, of lessening their dependence on guidance by fundamentalist imams with their vested interest in keeping their flock in a physical as well as spiritual ghetto. A backlash against fundamentalism among Muslim communities should not be ruled out; it has happened in most religions. But there should be no doubt about it: Even if a moderate Islam prevails, Europe will no longer be the same.

The policy of the secular forces in Europe will be based on a certain amount of appeasement, however difficult it may be for many to accept this. "Appeasement" is a term in disrepute—rightly so, in view of its historical connotation going back to the 1930s. But as nations have failed to take a strong stand that might have prevented the current crisis when it was still possible, what are the alternatives now, as immigrants of Muslim background become the majority in certain cities, regions, and subsequently perhaps even entire countries? A binational state perhaps? But this has not worked too well even in a country like Belgium. Or perhaps a united Europe in which the emphasis is no longer on the nation-state? There are, at present, no answers to these questions.

It means, among other things, refraining from criticizing the basic beliefs and practices of the other side; if a religion has 1.2 billion adherents, it is not advisable to talk openly and candidly about its negative aspects. Quantity, as Marx said, becomes a new quality. Some believe that the quaint observation of Prince Charles—how the Muslim critique of materialism helped him to rediscover the sacred Islamic spirituality—could be a model for the peacemakers on how to make friends and influence people in an age of tensions. A certain amount of self-censorship is already practiced by Western politicians and media, and there may be more of it in the future, such as the decision of a European television network not to screen a program about the situation of persecuted Christians in the Arab world and Pope Benedict XVI's expressions of regret (but no formal apology) following a speech he made in Bavaria in September 2006 in which he quoted a medieval Christian emperor's harsh characterization of Islam. In the same month, a Berlin opera house canceled plans to perform Mozart's *Idomeneo* for fear of what police called an incalculable risk of offending Muslim sensibilities (in a scene added by the director, the king of Crete,

Idomeneo, carries the severed heads of Jesus, Muhammad, Buddha, and Poseidon onstage and places each on a stool).

The case of Hirsi Ali could be a portent of the shape of things to come. This Somali woman who found refuge in Holland turned into a bitter critic of such Islamic practices as the genital mutilation of women, of which she was a victim. She eventually became a member of the Dutch parliament and appeared on *Time* magazine's list of the one hundred most influential persons in the world. But all this did not prevent a Dutch court in 2006 from deciding that she must leave her apartment in Amsterdam because her presence constituted a danger to her Dutch neighbors who had complained, arguing that they were not their brother's or sister's keeper; some went further and argued she was disturbing the peace and should be removed. Eventually, following a media campaign against her, she was forced to leave the country.

Taqi'a (roughly translated as dissimulation or pretending, also known as *ketman* in Old Persian) has long been used in extreme situations in the Muslim world, and it may be used by non-Muslims in certain circumstances. A new Machiavelli may be needed for practicing coexistence with radical political religions in the age of democracy. It is not an admirable practice, but it may save lives. Macaulay's essay on Machiavelli (1850) could be a starting point for reflection. *Qui nescit dissimulare, nescit regnare,* which (freely translated) means "He who does not know to dissimulate has no business being in politics." It means expressing not only understanding but also respect and even admiration toward a civilization and way of life basically alien to one's own values. The non-Muslim residents of the major Dutch cities, and subsequently of cities in Germany and elsewhere, will be well advised to acquire a working knowledge of Turkish or Arabic, just as the residents of Southern California and some southwestern states in the United

States have acquired a smattering of Spanish. The (London) *Times Atlas of the World* identifies Germany's currency as the euro and its language as German and Turkish; a premature statement, perhaps, but it could be true thirty years from now.

It also means a more nuanced approach by European authorities toward the Muslim communities in their midst, which, as has been stressed time and again, are anything but monolithic. There is no reason that the European authorities should treat the Muslims as if they were an integrated whole, which they have never been. The British example of dealing with the "moderate fundamentalists" as if these were the only authentic representatives of the Muslim community has not been a great success since the policy strengthened the anti-Western elements. Governments and local authorities should deal with all kinds of Muslim groups. Berber interests are by no means identical with Algerian; Turks and Kurds, not to mention Pakistanis and Moroccans, are of different backgrounds and have different group interests, which the authorities should consider, rather than negotiating only with leaders, often self-appointed, claiming to speak on behalf of the whole Muslim community, which in reality consists of disparate groups.

The decisive importance of education has been emphasized in these pages time and time again. Yet it is precisely in this field that the German approach has been least successful. According to alarming reports, normal teaching has virtually broken down in some Berlin schools frequented by emigrant children from Muslim countries. The schools have become a blackboard jungle of Arabs fighting Turks, Turks combating Kurds, Muslims versus emigrants from Russia and the Balkans, and everyone against the Germans.

Could it have been any different? The Muslim children come from patriarchal families, likely to be beaten for even light violations of the strict rules prevailing. Their encounter with progressive education must have been a cultural shock. The teachers know little about Islam and its way of life, and their antiauthoritarian training does not help in such an encounter. The spokeswoman of the Türkische Bund in Berlin (Eren Ünsal) has stressed that a certain measure of authority on the part of school and teachers was absolutely essential. A young Indian remembering his days at a school in Ealing, London, has written about their poor and helpless teachers, fresh faced, idealistic, who had read Marx and Malcolm X and had taken an elective course on postcolonial theory at a polytechnic institute. Desperate to sympathize with the persecution of their pupils, they were knocked dead by their indifference and rampant misbehavior. "We ate them alive at the first sign of guilt-ridden middle-class weakness" (*The Times,* London, April 9, 2006). Teachers in Berlin have suggested the closure of schools that are no longer under control. But with all the sympathy for the children's uphill struggle and the enormous difficulties they face, the question arises whether a less antiauthoritarian approach might have shown better results.

The situation in the Paris *banlieues* is not much better. The French authorities made special efforts over the last decade to improve education in the *banlieues:* There is a program called Second Chance for those trying to catch up at a later age, there are schools classified ZEP *(zone d'éducation prioritaire)* and ZUS *(zone urbaine sensible)* where special conditions are given, and there are schemes for the prevention of violence at school. And yet, with all this, the results are not impressive. The number of dropouts is several times higher than elsewhere, and the achievements of many pupils are poor.

What could be the solution? Send them to the soccer grounds, pay for their education in Turkey or Japan, or introduce boot-camp-style military discipline? Perhaps a Baden-Powell is needed to establish a new Boy Scout movement, but it is feared that if such a person should arise, he will be a radical Islamist. Concessions have to be considered. What should be the curriculum in state schools? There have been questions from the immigrant communities about whether Dutch children of Muslim origin should be taught about Rembrandt—who, after all, was not part of their tradition. Should young Muslims in Italy have to study the Renaissance, all kind of paintings of saints and madonnas of another religion, or the works of Dante, who wrote nasty things about the Prophet Muhammad?

Goethe said nice things about the common features of the Orient and Occident and he also wrote the *West-östlicher Divan* (West-Eastern divan), but he is not part of Turkish history. However, why should children of Moroccan origin in the Netherlands be taught the history of the Ottoman empire, which means little to them? It will not be easy to find common denominators. An educator at the London School of Economics, Iftikar Ahmed, pondering the low grades of children from Muslim families in British schools, put part of the blame on the fact that they were spending too much time learning the Holy Koran by heart in mosque schools and had no time for doing their homework. Nor could they identify with their non-Muslim teachers; special Muslim schools were needed to improve the situation. Will the situation improve with time? Investigations in Germany have shown that the second generation of pupils from Muslim families is in fact doing worse than the earlier generation. But what would be the religious-political orientation of separate Muslim schools? Would they not perpetuate the divisions in society? Nor would an improvement in the education of young people of a Muslim background solve their problems unless jobs could be found for them after graduation.

But how far should appeasement go? A British observer, Timothy Garton Ash, has expressed his belief that ultimately whether Muslim citizens will begin to feel at home in Europe will depend on the personal attitude and the behavior of hundreds of millions of their fellow Europeans. This seems to be based on the assumption that the Muslims' ambitions do not go further than "feeling at home," which cannot, however, be taken for granted. Ash rightly criticized the version of multiculturalism that goes, "You respect my taboos and I'll respect yours," noting that if one puts all the taboos of all the cultures together there is not much left one can talk freely about. But this is precisely one of the main bones of contention: Radical Islamists, with their emphasis on jihad, want immunity from criticism and any negative comments, whereas they feel no such immunity should be given to other religions and cultures. In brief, self-censorship, tact, and similar half measures on the part of European societies may not be sufficient. For appeasement to be successful it may have to go considerably further, praising the beauty of Islam and the justice of the sharia, stressing that there is very much that the West (having lost its spiritual moorings) can learn from Muslim spirituality, also accepting the complaints that Muslims have been victims all along and that their grievances are justified and that the West has to make amends.

Whether a policy of massive appeasement will succeed is uncertain. It could perhaps lead to an uneasy peaceful coexistence, but it would mean a near total transformation of European civilization. It might be unacceptable for a majority of Europeans, who fear for their status and their identity in a future Europe. It is against this background that conflicts are bound to arise. Tolerance toward minorities has not been one of the distinguishing features of Muslim societies in modern history; the Armenians have not fared well in Turkey, nor the Copts in Egypt, nor the Bahai in Iran, nor even the Shiites or the Ahmadiya and Ismailiya in Pakistan, even though they are Muslims. The status of Christians in Indonesia, one of the most tolerant Muslim countries, is still problematic, and so is that of the Chinese in Malaysia. If this does not change in the course of the coming decades, the prospects for peaceful coexistence in Europe will be dim. One-sided tolerance, experience has shown, does not work.

Turkey to the Rescue?

WHAT IF TURKEY were to join the European Union?

This issue has not been discussed so far in my review; after some initial enthusiasm there has been growing skepticism on both sides. There was substantial support in Turkey for going into the European Union—some 80 percent, more than in most countries that belong to the European Union—but support declined as time went by. There was support in Britain and France but substantial opposition in Germany, Austria, and some other countries. Many Germans suspected that the primary loyalty of the Turks living in the European Union would be toward their country of origin rather than to the country of adoption, but this would be the case irrespective of whether Turkey joined the European Union or not. It was also clear that, given the demographic trends, Turkey would be the most populous country in Europe, strengthening the Islamic factor inside the European Union.

Inside Turkey, declining enthusiasm was caused partly by a growing nationalist mood as well as an impressive economic performance—annual growth of almost 10 percent. But with all this, per capita income in Turkey is still little more than $4,000, much less than in other European countries, and it was feared that this would cause a further massive influx of Turks into Europe.

Furthermore, the political and social conditions imposed by the European Union on all member states (but implicitly above all concerning Turkey) were a matter of concern to many Turks. Entering the European Union would cause hardships to Turkish agriculture (one-third of Turks are employed in this sector of the economy) as well as shop owners. It would also affect Turkish domestic policy, as with relations toward minorities such as Kurds.

Could Turkey be a bridge toward the Muslim world and, as such, be a potential partner in moderating relations between a secular Europe and the Muslim communities? This is perhaps the decisive issue; for decades, since Kemal Atatürk, the founder and first president (1923–38) of modern Turkey, the nation had been moving toward modernization and secularism. But during the last decade or two Islamism—or, to be precise, a mixture of Islamism and Panturkism—has been gaining strength, and with it a basic anti-Western orientation. True, the secular forces inside Turkey are still much stronger than in the Arab world, and even the Turkish Islamists, the Justice and Development Party (AKP), were not remotely as extreme as the Muslim Brotherhood—the very fact that the AKP supported going into Europe pointed in this direction. (It also recently opened a museum of modern Western art in Istanbul.) However, the situation in Turkey seems unpredictable, and a country turning away from the legacy of Kemal, the founder of modern Turkey, was the last thing the European Union wanted.

THIS, THEN, IS A PICTURE of Europe in the first decade of the new century. It is a picture of gradual decline that offers little comfort to Euro-optimists. Future historians may well be at a loss to understand why the sorry state of affairs was realized only late in the day, despite the fact that all the major trends mentioned in this brief study—demography, the stalling of the movement toward European unity, and the crisis of the welfare state—had appeared well before the turn of the century. Had it not been for the murder of filmmaker Theo van Gogh in 2004, a few Dutch intellectuals would have written articles about Holland's domestic difficulties with immigrants, but there would not have been a national debate about what suddenly appeared an existential issue.

The decline of the Roman empire has been discussed for centuries and it could well be that the discussion about the decline of Europe will last as long. Why was it ignored for so long? In part this could be explained as the result of the fixation in Europe on America—America as a model and as a deterrent, America as a rival, opponent, and ally—at the cost of ignoring the rest of the world. But there must have been other causes, and they will be discussed for a long time to come. There are many fascinating problems. Was the decline perhaps inevitable? Was it reversible? If so, at what stage did it become irreversible?

Decline very often proceeds not as quickly as feared; there are usually retarding circumstances. But it is also true that, for better or worse, the pulse of history is beating quicker in our time than in the Middle Ages. The collapse of the Soviet Union, for instance, occurred very quickly. As hard as Mr. Putin and his colleagues are trying to recover at least part of what has been lost, the odds of succeeding are against them.

There is a danger, after the threats to Europe have been neglected for so long, of throwing up our hands in despair and accepting with resignation its future role as a museum of world history and civilization preaching the importance of morality in world affairs to a nonexistent audience.

Decline offers challenges that ought to be taken up even if

there is no certainty of success. No one could say with any confidence what problems the powers that now appear to be on the ascendancy will face in the years to come. There could be great dangers facing all mankind in the decades to come that cannot be discerned clearly as yet. Even if Europe's decline is now irreversible, there is no reason that it should become a collapse. There is, however, a precondition: facing realities at long last, something that has been postponed in many parts of Europe to this day. The debate should be about which of Europe's traditions and values can still be saved, not about Europe as a shining example for all mankind, the moral superpower of the twenty-first century. The age of delusions is over. Anyone who doubts this should take a guided tour through Neukölln or La Courneuve or the center of Bradford: not the best places, not the worst, but a fair indication of the shape of things to come. These places, too, are bound to change, but it will be a very slow process and the outcome will be a Europe quite different from the one we have known.

Bibliography

Demography

Birg, Herwig. *Die demographische Zeitenwende.* Munich, 2003.

Chesnais, J. C. *La transition démographique.* Paris, 1986.

Cohen, R. *The Encyclopedia of Immigrant Groups.* Cambridge, 1995.

Coleman, D. (ed.). *Europe's Population in the 1990s.* Oxford, 1996.

Demenyi, Paul. "Population Policy Dilemmas in Europe at the Dawn of the Twenty-first Century" in *Population and Development Review.* March 2003.

Council of Europe. *Recent Demographic Developments.* Strassbourg, n.d.

United Nations (ed.). *World Population Prospects. The 1998 Revisions. The 2001 Revisions.* n.d.

United Nations (ed.). *World Population in 2300.* n.d.

Europe (General)

Bawer, Bruce. *While Europe Slept: How Radical Islam Is Destroying the West from Within.* New York, 2006.

Cesari, Jocelyne. *When Islam and Democracy Meet.* New York, 2004.

Fetzer, Joel, and Christopher Sper. *Muslims and the State in Britain, France and Germany.* New York, 2004.

Kepel, Gilles. *Les banlieues de l'Islam.* Paris, 1987.

Klausen, Jytte. *The Islamic Challenge.* New York, 2006.

Lewis, Bernard. *Islam and the West.* London, 1993.

Ramadan, Tariq. *Western Muslims and the Future of Islam.* New York, 2003.

Rath, Jan, et al. *Western Europe and Its Islam.* Leiden, 2001.

Roy, Olivier. *Globalized Islam.* New York, 2005.

Spalek, B. (ed.). *Islam, Crime and Criminal Justice.* Cullompton, 2002.

Spuler-Stegemann, Ursula. *Muslime in Deutschland.* Freiburg, 2002.

Tibi, Bassam. *Europa ohne Identität?* Munich, 1998.

Wiktorowicz, Quinton. *Radical Islam Rising.* London, 2005.

France

Baverez, Nicolas. *La France qui tombe.* Paris, 2003.

Beaud, Stéphane, and Michel Pialoux. *Violences urbaines, violence sociale.* Paris, 2003.

Brenner, E. *Les territoires perdus de la République.* Paris, 2002.

Burgat, F. *L'Islamisme en face.* Paris, 2002.

Cites 2003. L'Islam en France. Paris, 2004.

Fourest, Caroline. *Frère Tariq.* Paris, 2003.

———. *La tentation obscurantiste.* Paris, 2005.

Gaspard, Françoise, and Farhad Khosrokavar. *Le foulard et la République.* Paris, 1995

Goaziou, Veronique le, et al. *Quand les banlieues brûlent.* Paris, 2006.

Jelen, Christian. *La guerre des rues.* Paris, 1999.
Juillard, Jacques. *Le malheur français.* Paris, 2006.
Landau, Paul. *Sabre et Coran.* Paris, 2005.
Lawrence, Jonathan, and Justin Vaisse. *Integrating Islam.* Washington, D.C., 2006.
Merlin, Pierre. *Les banlieues.* Paris, 1999.
Mermet, Gerard (ed.). *Francoscopie.* Paris, 2006.
oumma.com.
Sfeir, A. *Les reseaux d'Allah.* Paris, 2001.
Ternisien, Xavier. *La France des mosques.* Paris, 2004.
Tribalat, Michel. *De l'immigration à l'assimilation.* Paris, 1996.
Weil, Patrick. *La France et ses étrangers.* Paris, 1991.

Islamist Terrorism in Europe

Bundesnachrichtendienst. *Verfassungsschutzbericht.* Berlin, 2005.
Khosravar, Farhad. *Suicide Bombers.* London, 2005.
Marret, Jean-Luc. *Les fabriques du jihad.* Paris, 2005.
McDermott, Terry. *Perfect Soldiers.* New York, 2005.
Moniquet, Claude. *Le jihad.* Paris, 2004.
Vidino, Lorenzo. *Al Qaeda in Europe.* Amherst, 2005.

United Kingdom

Abbas, Taher (ed.). *Muslim Britain.* London, 2005.
Ballard, Roger. *Desh Pradesh.* London, 1994.
Baumann, Gerd. *Contesting Culture.* Cambridge, 1996.
Dalrymple, Theodore. *Life at the Bottom.* Chicago, 2001.
Dench, Geoff, et al. *The New East End.* London, 2006.
Jacobson, Jessica. *Islam in Transition.* London, 1998.
Joly, Daniele. *Britannia's Crescent.* Aldershot, 1995.
Lewis, Philip. *Islamic Britain.* London, 1994.
Modood, Tariq. *Multicultural Politics.* Edinburgh, 2005.
Philips, Melanie. *Londonistan.* London, 2006.
Thomas, Dominique. *Le Londonistan.* Paris, 2003.

Germany

Bott, Peter, et al. *Türkische Jugendliche.* Hohengelen, 1991.

Heitmeyer, W., et al. *Verlockender Fundamentalismus.* Frankfurt, 1998.

Kelek, Necla. *Islam im Alltag.* Munich, 2002.

———. *Die verlorenen Söhne.* Cologne, 2006.

Lachmann, Guenter. *Tödliche Toleranz: Die Muslime und unsere offene Gesellschaft.* Munich, 2005.

Lemmen, Thomas. *Islamische Organisationen in Deutschland.* Bonn, 2000.

Luft, Stefan. *Ausländerpolitik in Deutschland.* Gräfelfing, 2003.

Raddatz, Hans Peter. *Die türkische Gefahr?* Munich, 2004.

Rohe, Mathias. *Der Islam—Alltagskonflikte.* Freiburg, 2001.

Schiffauer, Werner. *Die Gottesmänner.* Frankfurt, 2000.

Sen, Faruk, and Hayrettin Aydin. *Islam in Deutschland.* Munich, 2005.

Spuler-Stegemann, Ursula. *Muslime in Deutschland.* Freiburg, 2002.

Tibi, Bassim. *Islamische Zuwanderung.* Stuttgart, 2002.

Tietze, Nikola. *Türkische Identitäten.* Hamburg, 2001.

European Union

Archer, Clive, and Fiona Butler. *The European Community.* New York, 1992.

Baun, Michael. *A Wider Europe.* Lanham, Md., 2000.

Bitsch, Marie Therese. *Histoire de la construction européenne de 1945 à nos jours.* Paris, 1998.

Council of Europe (Web site), www.coe.int.

Crafts, N. F. R., and G. Toniolo (eds.). *Economic Growth in Europe Since 1945.* Cambridge, 1996.

Croci, Osvaldo. *European Unity: A Bibliography* (current, Internet).

Denman, M. J. *The Origins and the Development of the European Union 1945–95.* London, 1996.

European Union (official Web site), www.europa.eu.int.

European Commission (Web site), www.europa.euint/com.

Europe Council of Ministers (Web site), www.europa.ue.eu.int.

European Voice (Brussels).

Farell, Mary, et al. *European Integration in the 21st Century.* London, 2002.

Gehler, Michael. *Europa: Von der Utropie zum Euro.* Frankfurt, 2002.

Gillingham, John. *European Integration 1950–2003.* Cambridge, 2003.

Gruner, Wolf D., and Wichard Woyke. *Europa Lexikon.* Munich, 2004.

Hayward, Jack, and Edward Page. *Governing the New Europe.* Durham, N.C., 1995.

Jones, Eric. *The European Miracle.* Cambridge, 2003.

Judt, Tony. *PostWar.* New York, 2005.

Kagan, Robert. "Power and Weakness" in *Policy Review.* June 2002.

McCormick, John (ed.). *The European Union: Politics and Policies.* Cambridge, Mass., 2004.

Milward, Alan. *The Reconstruction of Western Europe.* London, 1992.

Moravcsik, Andrew. *The Choice for Europe.* New York, 1998.

NATO (Web site), www.nato.int.

Nielsen, Brent F., and Alexander Stubb. *The European Union.* Boulder, Co., 2003.

Schimmelfennig, Frank *The EU, NATO and the Integration of Europe.* Cambridge, 2003.

Torbioern, Kjell. *Destination Europe.* Manchester, 2003.

Europe—Economic Giant?

Baverez, Nicolas. *La France qui tombe.* Paris, 2004.

———. *Nouveau monde, vieille France.* Paris, 2006.

Buchsteiner, Jochen. *Die Stunde der Asiaten.* Hamburg, 2005.

Butterwegge, Christoph. *Krise und Zukunft des Sozialstaates.* Wiesbaden, 2005.

Baily, Martin, and Jacob Kirkegaard. *Tranforming the European Economy.* Washington, DC, 2004.

Einhorn, Eric, and John Logue. *Modern Welfare States.* New York, 1989.

Eurobarometer.

Eurostat Comparative Performance Statistics (Web site), europa.eu.int.

Hüfner, Martin. *Europa, die Macht von Morgen.* Munich, 2006.

Jones, Eric. *The European Miracle.* Cambridge, 2003.

Kalff, Donald. *Unamerican Business.* New York, 2002.

Kupchan, Charles. *The End of the America Era.* New York, 2002.

Leonard, Mark. *Why Europe Will Run the 21st Century.* London, 2005.

Miegel, Meinhard. *Epochenwende.* Berlin, 2005.

OECD. Paris annual country reports.

Olson, Mancur. *The Rise and Decline of Nations: Economic Growth, Stagflation, and Social Rigidities.* New Haven, 1982.

Ottenheimer, Ghislaine. *Nos vaches sacrées.* Paris, 2006.

Pond, Elizabeth. *The Rebirth of Europe.* Washington, D.C., 1999.

Razin, Assaf, and Efraim Sadka. *The Decline of the Welfare State.* Cambridge, Mass., 2005.

Rifkin, Jeremy. *The American Dream.* New York, 2004.

Smith, Timothy. *France in Crisis.* Cambridge, 2004.

Sinn, Hans Werner. *1st Deutschland noch zu retten?* Essen, 2004.

Steingart, Gabor. *Deutschland: Der Abschied eines Superstars.* Munich, 2004.

Russia

Baker, Peter, and Susan Glaser. *Vladimir Putin's Russia and the End of the Revolution.* New York, 2005.

Blotsky, Oleg. *Vladimir Putin: Doroga k vlasti.* Moscow, 2002.

Evangelista, M. *The Chechen Wars.* Washington, D.C., 2002.

Golubchikov, Yu, et al. *Islamisatsiya Rossii: Trevozhnie szenarii budushshevo.* Moscow, 2005.

Hoffman, David. *The Oligarchs.* New York, 2001.

Johnson's Russia List/Center for Defense Information. http://www.cdi.org/russia/johnson/default.cfm.

McFaul, Michael, et al. *Between Dictatorship and Democracy.* Washington, D.C., 2004.

Politkovskaya, Anna. *Putin's Russia.* New York, 2005.

Putin, Vladimir. *Ot pervovo litsa.* Moscow, 2000.

Sakwa, Richard. *Putin.* London, 2004.

Satter, David. *Darkness at Dawn.* New Haven, 2003.

Shevtsova, Lilia. *Putin's Russia.* Washington, D.C., 2005.

Telen, Lyudmilla. *Pokolenie Putina.* Moscow, 2004.

Reflections on the Future of Europe

Belaid, Chakri. *Banlieue: Lendemains de révolte.* Paris, 2006.

Birg, Herwig. *Die Weltbevölkerung.* Munich, 2003.

Bondy-Gendrot, Sophie. *Minorities in European Cities.* London, 2002.

Cesari, Jocelyn. *Islam in France.* London, 2002.

—— (ed). *Mosque Conflicts in Western Europe,* special issue of *Journal of Ethnic and Migration Studies.* November 2005.

Conzen, Peter. *Fanatismus: Psychoanalyse eines unheimlichen Phänomens.* Stuttgart, 2005.

Council of Europe. *The Future of European Population.* Strassbourg, 1992.

Hagedorn, John. "The Global Impact of Gangs" in *Journal of Contemporary Criminal Justice.* May 2005.

Hall, Tarqin. *Salaam Brick Lane.* London, 2005.

Kaha, Ayan. *Sicher in Kreuzberg.* Istanbul, 2000.

Percy, Andrew. *Ethnicity and Victimization.* London, 1998.

Pew Research Center. *An Uncertain Road: Muslims and the Future of Europe.* Philadelphia, 2005.

Posner, Richard A. *Catastrophe: Risk and Response.* New York, 2004.

Puetz, Robert. *Unternehmer türkischer Herkunft.* Berlin, 2004.

Savage, Timothy. "Europe and Islam" in *Washington Quarterly.* Summer 2004.

Swedenburg, Ted. "Islamic Hip-Hop vs. Islamophobia" in Tony Mitchell, ed., *Global Noise: Rap and Hip-Hop Outside the USA.* New York, 2002.

White, Jenny B. "Turks in Germany: Overview of the Literature" in *Middle East Studies Association Bulletin.* July 1995.

Index